BIG BETHEL

BIG BETHEL

The First Battle

JOHN V. QUARSTEIN

Charleston  London

THE
History
PRESS

Published by The History Press
Charleston, SC 29403
www.historypress.net

Front cover: *Winthrop's Final Assault at Bethel Church*, Gail Duke, 2011.
Back cover: *top*: Major General John Bankhead Magruder, CSA. *Bottom*: Brigadier General Abram Duryee, USA.

First published 2011

Manufactured in the United States

ISBN 978.1.60949.354.7

Library of Congress Cataloging-in-Publication Data

Quarstein, John V.
Big Bethel : the first battle / John V. Quarstein.
p. cm.
Includes bibliographical references and index.
ISBN 978-1-60949-354-7
1. Big Bethel, Battle of, Va., 1861. I. Title.
E472.14.Q37 2011
973.7'31--dc22
2011013959

Contents

Acknowledgements

Big Bethel: The First Battle presents the series of events on the Virginia Peninsula that culminated in the 10 June 1861 Battle of Big Bethel. This is the story of how the Civil War evolved from passionate rhetoric to vicious combat. Even though the engagement's luster would pale and be surpassed by much bloodier battles, it would be well remembered by those who fought at Big Bethel. It was, indeed, an awakening to the grim reality of war. Therefore, this volume is dedicated to the nineteen men who perished along the banks of Brick Kiln Creek—men like Henry Lawson Wyatt, John T. Greble and Theodore Winthrop, who left behind a record of bravery, all too often repeated throughout the next four years.

Big Bethel first interested me when I was growing up on Fort Monroe. It was marvelous to be there during the Civil War Centennial, especially when Dr. Chester Bradley, then curator of The Casemate Museum, befriended me. He told me stories about the battle as we looked at Lieutenant Greble's frock coat. This was amazing, allowing me to become part of this officer's story. I knew then that I would one day write a book about Big Bethel.

Fast-forward thirty years. I had embarked upon some major Civil War preservation initiatives on the Peninsula. My success with these endeavors and my ability to articulate Hampton Roads' dramatic Civil War heritage prompted my good friend and historic preservation patron Dorothy Rouse Bottom to request that I write a history of Big Bethel. I immediately agreed. However, after completing my research, my focus shifted to authoring books about ironclads and the Peninsula Campaign of 1862. Yet Big Bethel never left my mind. Nor could it, as my son, John Moran, would constantly ask me, "So, how is Big Bethel?" The Bethel story just kept building within me. Consequently, ten years later, when the Hampton Civil War Sesquicentennial Committee initiated an effort to preserve the last portion of the Big Bethel Battlefield, I realized the time had come to produce this volume.

The entire text was handwritten on a clipboard I used in the early 1960s and with my Parker Sonnet fountain pen. My text was transposed into a working document by Nancy Jones of the Pickett-Buchanan Chapter UDC and by my assistant, Heidi Walsh. J. Michael Moore, historian at Lee Hall Mansion, served as my primary reader. Michael also helped, ably supported by Dave Johnson of The Casemate Museum, to gather the lion's share of the images needed to illustrate this book. Other photos, paintings, prints and sketches are from treasured collections held by the Virginia War Museum, The Casemate Museum, Hampton History Museum, Museum of the Confederacy, U.S. Military History Institute, John Moran Quarstein, Patrick Schroeder, Crickett Bauer Messman and Timothy Messman and the late Brian C. Pohanka. The front cover is a scene from an original painting by the ever-so-talented Gail Duke, who was commissioned to create a mural documenting the dramatic final moments of the battle. She did an outstanding job. Of course, the talented wordsmith and editor Julie Murphy of Circle C Communications must also be noted for her excellent and exacting work. As ever, she made sure that my words reached beyond the norm to tell the Bethel tale. Julie, a Tar Heel and member of the Bridgers Family Association, felt close ties to this story as she read of Captain John Bridgers and the Edgecombe Guards.

My appreciation must also be extended to Thomas B. Hunter of the Onondaga Historical Museum & Research Center for providing me detailed information about the Syracuse Zouaves. Of special note is Patrick Schroeder, who surveyed my text and was so gracious to enable me to reference Brian Pohanka's manuscript, *Red-legged Devils: History of the Fifth New York Volunteer Infantry: Duryee's Zouaves*. Patrick plans to publish this volume in 2012.

Big Bethel was written to support the ongoing effort to preserve and present the Big Bethel Battlefield. This preservation endeavor was aided by a wide variety of people. Many years ago, I took Sherry Greshamer of Bethel Chapter UDC to find the 1961 monument, long hidden in the woods of

Langley Air Force Base. I never saw anyone so happy to find a monument, yet she was. She told me then, in 2006, that something must be done to make Big Bethel accessible. Accordingly, when I started establishing partnerships to establish a battlefield experience, the Bethel Chapter was the first group to offer support. Eventually, numerous groups like the Vermont Hemlocks, Raleigh CWRT, Hampton Civil War Sesquicentennial Committee, City of Hampton, Hampton History Museum Association, Virginia Civil War Trails, Langley Air Force Base, Pickett-Buchanan Chapter UDC, Hampton CVB, Chicago CWRT and Virginia Peninsula Chamber of Commerce Leadership Institute Alumni all joined together to help me create the battlefield park and interpretive trail, install the Vermont Monument, preserve the last section of the one-gun battery and relocate two older Bethel Chapter monuments into this park. So many individuals from these organizations—Jim Wilson, Christine Gergely, Adanna Davis, Bruce Sturk, Sallie Grant-DiVenuti, Jim Tormey and Bob Allsbrook—really made a difference. Of course, I truly thank several others for making the extra effort to ensure success. My friend Dr. Bill Minsinger took the initiative for creating the Vermont Monument, and my former Leadership Institute student Loline Otzelberger helped gather and organize the volunteer team that was required. Charles Hawks of the Raleigh CWRT also must be given great accolades for helping to raise money.

Introduction

Virginia's Hampton Roads region is home to so many historical firsts. Many of these great moments in time occurred during the Civil War. The Contraband of War decision and the duel between the ironclads USS *Monitor* and CSS *Virginia* (*Merrimack*) influenced the conflict's outcome and events that followed. One of the Civil War firsts that is often overlooked is the 10 June 1861 Battle of Big Bethel. While virtually a minor skirmish in comparison to the later vicious battles that epitomized the war, Big Bethel was the first time that Union and Confederate soldiers engaged in open combat. The clash also caused some of the war's first combat casualties, including the first Union soldier killed, the death of the first West Pointer and Regular Army officer and the mortal wounding of the first Confederate infantryman. Big Bethel was a precursor to the bloody battles to follow until the war's end in 1865.

The Union's ability to maintain control of Fort Monroe during the secession crisis provided the Federals with an important strategic toehold in Confederate territory. Not only could Fort Monroe, located on the very tip of the Virginia Peninsula, support the operations down the Southern coast of the North Atlantic Blockading Squadron, but it also provided a springboard for a Union advance against the Confederate capital at Richmond. Fort Monroe, known as the Key to the South, quickly overflowed with Federal soldiers. When Major General Benjamin Franklin Butler assumed command, he sought to use the Peninsula approach to strike against Richmond. By early June 1861, the Federals had occupied Hampton and had built two additional camps, Camp Butler and Camp Hamilton. Butler's soldiers were ranging beyond Newmarket Creek, and the Confederates appeared to be unable to counter the Federals aggressions.

When John Bankhead Magruder was assigned to take command at Yorktown, he immediately surveyed the Peninsula to ascertain how to guard this approach against Richmond. Magruder, a bon vivant and raconteur, nicknamed "Prince John" for his courtly manners and lavish dress, was an 1830 West Point graduate and a hero of the Mexican War. He knew that he needed time to build a comprehensive defensive system to defend the Peninsula against Federal aggressions. He selected Big Bethel Church, located at the Hampton-York Highway's crossing of the northwest branch of the Back River, to bait Butler into an attack. Colonel Daniel Harvey Hill, another West Pointer and hero of the Mexican War, commander of the 1st North Carolina, assumed a leadership role at Big Bethel instructing his men, along with the Richmond Howitzers, Wythe Rifles, 3rd Virginia and Montague's Battalion, to construct earthworks.

The Federals, meanwhile, had not been idle. Butler continued to receive additional reinforcements and began probing the surrounding countryside. On 7 June and again the next day, Federal scouting units, such as Colonel Max Weber's Turner Rifles, clashed with Confederates near Newmarket Bridge. The no-man's land between the Back River's northern and southern beaches was now hotly contested. Butler became aware of the Confederate presence at Little Bethel and Big Bethel. The Union general was convinced that he must strike out and destroy these Confederate troops. A night march was planned using troops from Camp Hamilton and Camp Butler to make a surprise attack upon the Confederates.

Everything went wrong. The Union maps were outdated, and the plan failed from almost the very beginning. When the Union troops junctured near Little Bethel, the 7th New York fired into the 3rd New York. It was the first friendly fire incident of the Civil War and alerted the Confederates to the Federal advance.

Brigadier General Ebenezer Peirce, in command of the 4,400 Union troops involved in this operation, held a "council of war." Although the Federals realized that the element of surprise had been lost, Peirce ordered the troops to march on to Big Bethel.

Magruder had arrived at Big Bethel on 9 June and assumed overall command of the 1,400 Confederates. Captain Judson Kilpatrick of the

Duryee's Zouaves (5th New York) was the first to arrive on the battlefield. After an exchange of artillery fire between Major George Wythe Randolph's Richmond Howitzers and Lieutenant John T. Greble's battery, the Union launched several piecemeal attacks against the Confederate one-gun battery. Even though the Federals were able to capture the battery, briefly, they were quickly forced to retire. One final assault against the main Confederate redoubt was organized by Major Theodore Winthrop. Winthrop, a Yale graduate and military secretary to General Butler, led elements of the 1st Vermont and 4th Massachusetts across a ford. The initial attack was repulsed by the 1st North Carolina. When Winthrop tried to rally his men, he was shot and killed by an African American, Sam Ashe, serving with the 1st North Carolina. The battle was over, and the Federals rushed to safety beyond Newmarket Creek Bridge.

Big Bethel was a complete failure for the Union. D.H. Hill commented that his soldiers "seemed to enjoy it as much as boys do rabbit-shooting." The Federals lost a total of seventy-six men: eighteen killed, fifty-three wounded and five missing. Both Butler and Peirce were blamed for the defeat. The Northern press called the Union troops courageous, as "they fought both friend and foe alike with equal resolution." Meanwhile, the Confederates rejoiced over their victory and proclaimed all the Southern soldiers as heroes. Robert E. Lee wrote to Magruder and expressed "my great satisfaction at the gallant conduct of the troops under your command and approbation of dispositions made by you, resulting as they did, in the route of the enemy."

The 10 June 1861 Battle of Big Bethel is noted for being the Civil War's first land battle. The engagement blocked the first Union advance against Richmond. The battle lines were drawn on the Virginia Peninsula, and troop positions would remain virtually the same until April 1862. It was a small engagement compared to the death and destruction to follow during the next few years. Bethel was, nevertheless, the first significant action of the war and caused an immediate sensation in both the North and the South. The defeat helped the Federals realize that their men needed better training and leadership. The Confederate victory was overstated, breeding a false sense of Southern invincibility.

As the years began to slip by after the war, many Virginia Peninsula residents sought to honor those who served at Big Bethel. The first Confederate markers were erected in 1905. The Bethel Chapter UDC organized the installation of an obelisk in the Big Bethel churchyard, and the State of North Carolina installed a marker in Raleigh noting the spot where Henry

Lawson Wyatt was killed. When the Civil War Centennial was celebrated in 1961, the Bethel Chapter once again placed a memorial on the battlefield. Even though these monuments and memorials mark the hallowed place, they did not serve to preserve the battlefield, which was soon hidden by a reservoir, woodland, housing, shops and fences. Nevertheless, when the 150th anniversary of the battle approached, many Civil War Sesquicentennial advocates banded together to provide on-site interpretation, earthwork preservation and a new monument honoring Union soldiers who fought along the banks of Brick Kiln Creek.

Big Bethel is indeed an engagement that should be remembered. Several officers who fought at Bethel would eventually rise to general's rank. The nineteen men who died as a result of the battle should never be forgotten. Several of their stories need to be shared as a reminder of leadership and uncommon valor. The first Confederate infantryman to die in battle, Henry Lawson Wyatt, eventually would have four monuments installed to memorialize his service. Wyatt, of Company A, 1st North Carolina, achieved martyrdom as he had been mortally wounded by a shot through the forehead during a volunteer mission to "burn a house between the lines." "Too much praise," Magruder later commented, "cannot be bestowed upon the heroic soldier who we lost." Likewise, two Union officers must be especially remembered. Theodore Winthrop and John T. Greble were lionized for their valor and sacrifice in 1861; however, they are virtually forgotten today. Lieutenant Greble, who was killed near the battle's end while "nobly fighting his guns," was the first Regular Army officer and West Point graduate killed during the war. He had commanded his battery with distinction and was described as possessing "to a notable degree the two qualities needed at the time, namely, military skill and presence of mind in the face of the enemy." Major Theodore Winthrop, who was told by General Ben Butler to "Be Bold! Be Bold! But not too bold," almost won the day for the Union with his fateful heroism. These men fell at Bethel for causes they felt just and became symbols of the terrible cost of war.

There is an unseen battlefield
In every human breast
Where two opposing forces meet
And where they seldom rest...

Chapter 1

The Drama Begins

When Virginia left the Union on 17 April 1861, the Hampton Roads region was recognized as one of the most strategic locations within the commonwealth. On the south side, eight miles up the Elizabeth River, was Gosport Navy Yard. Gosport was the finest navy yard in the United States, containing a granite dry dock, ship houses, a foundry and a vast quantity of equipment, weapons and supplies. Across the harbor was the Virginia Peninsula. The Peninsula is a narrow strip of land formed by the Chesapeake Bay, York River, Hampton Roads and James River. Old Point Comfort was located at the very tip of the Peninsula, and following the War of 1812, the site was fortified. The fort, built from 1819 to 1834, was named Fort Monroe and became the largest moat-encircled masonry fortification in North America. Fort Monroe commanded the lower Chesapeake Bay and guarded the entrance to Hampton Roads. As the war clouds descended upon Virginia following the fall of Fort Sumter in Charleston Harbor, North and South alike sought to control these valuable military and naval assets.

Gosport immediately became the Confederate focus, as they needed the yard to create a navy. Accordingly, Brigadier General William Booth Taliaferro of the Virginia militia organized his meager resources and invested the yard on 18 April 1861. The next day, Taliaferro demanded that Flag Officer Charles Stewart McCauley surrender the yard to the "Sovereign State of Virginia." McCauley, a fifty-five-year naval veteran and heavy drinker, vacillated. His indecision prompted Union Secretary of the

Navy Gideon Welles to send a task force under the command of Flag Officer Hiram Paulding. Paulding left the Washington Navy Yard aboard the USS *Pawnee* and steamed to Old Point Comfort. He arrived in the afternoon of 20 April and embarked 350 men from the 3rd Massachusetts. This unit had just arrived to reinforce Fort Monroe.

Meanwhile, McCauley, who believed he was surrounded by far greater numbers, ordered the yard abandoned and destroyed. Every warship in the harbor, except the USS *Cumberland* and venerable USF *United States*, was set on fire, along with the ship houses. All Paulding could do was order his men to complete the destructive work. By 4:20 a.m., the Federals left Gosport. The *Pawnee* towed the *Cumberland*, which was followed by the gunboat *Yankee*. Gosport was seemingly in ruins, and by 6:15 a.m. on 21 April 1861, the Federal ships anchored off Fort Monroe.

While the yard appeared to be an utter wasteland, the Federals had left with such haste that the Confederates still found cause to rejoice. Much property was still intact, including the foundry, machine shop and granite dry dock; tons of supplies remained untouched by the blaze, including a

Old Point Comfort Lighthouse, 1860. *Courtesy of The Casemate Museum.*

total of 1,085 heavy cannon, many with carriages, a large number of shells and 250,000 pounds of gunpowder. Besides all of this equipment and weaponry, three warships—the *Merrimack*, *Germantown* and *Plymouth*—could be salvaged. The Richmond press gloated over the abundance of material and supplies stating, "We have enough to build a navy of iron-plated ships."[1]

Even though the Confederates had secured a great resource with their capture of Gosport Navy Yard, they did not have the ability to contest control of Fort Monroe. The Confederates lacked manpower, heavy guns, warships and time to besiege the fort. U.S. Army General in Chief Brevet Lieutenant General Winfield Scott immediately recognized the huge fort's importance to the Federal cause. Scott had great confidence in Fort Monroe's commanding officer, Lieutenant Colonel Justin Dimick, a highly loyal and skilled officer.

Dimick, an 1819 West Point graduate from Connecticut, was a forty-year veteran, brevetted for gallantry during the Seminole and Mexican Wars. He was in command of the only prewar Federal base in Virginia retained by the Union. While he had already detached troops from the fort's garrison by order of General Scott to reinforce Fort Sumter and Fort Pickens, major

Hancock Guards, 4th Massachusetts Infantry Regiment, 1861. *Courtesy of The Casemate Museum.*

improvements had been made to the fort years before, under the direction of Lieutenant Colonel René Eduard DeRussy. Nevertheless, Dimick concentrated on strengthening Fort Monroe, requesting more troops, rations and ordnance.

On 20 April 1861, Colonel David W. Wardrop's 3rd Massachusetts and Colonel Abner B. Packard's 4th Massachusetts arrived at Old Point Comfort. Ammunition and rations also were shipped to the fort. On 30 April, Scott advised Dimick that more equipment was en route and noted that "Fort Monroe is by far the most secure position in the possession of the U.S., against any attack that can be possibly made upon it, independent of the war vessels, the *Cumberland* and the *Niagara*, at hand, and approaching you."[2]

Scott realized that Fort Monroe was a critical key to Union victory. His long years of service made him recognize that these were two major approaches to the Confederate capital at Richmond. The overland route from Washington, D.C., was one such route; however, Scott observed that an advance from Fort Monroe toward Richmond was the most advantageous. Troops could march directly up the Peninsula against the Confederate

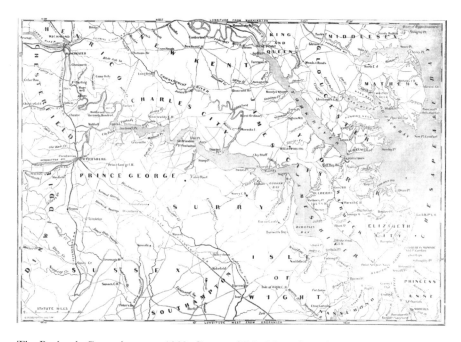

The Peninsula Campaign map, 1862. *Courtesy of John Moran Quarstein.*

capital as the U.S. Navy, using the James and York Rivers, could carry an army's supplies and support its flanks.

The Confederates also recognized the Peninsula as an avenue of approach against their capital and realized that Federal control of Fort Monroe meant that the Unionists would quickly use the fort as a base to control Tidewater Virginia. Consequently, on 27 April 1861, State Adjutant General Robert S. Garnett commissioned Benjamin Stoddert Ewell as a major and ordered him to begin organizing volunteers from James City, York, Elizabeth City and Warwick Counties for the defense of the Peninsula. Ewell, an 1832 graduate of the U.S. Military Academy and president of the College of William and Mary, had already established the Williamsburg Junior Guard in 1859 and sought to muster other militia units into a viable force. Furthermore, Ewell had to prepare his riverine flanks against any Federal naval movement as well as to create a defensive system blocking roads leading up the Peninsula to Richmond.

The Confederates were truly concerned about defending Virginia's waterways. In late April, navy Lieutenant Catesby Roger Jones arrived at Jamestown Island to establish a defensive work guarding the James River. He fortunately discovered that local landowner William Allen had arranged for eight thirty-two-pound guns to be sent to Jamestown and had already initiated construction of an earthwork. Jones, however, needed men; yet Ewell had none to give.

Meanwhile, Gloucester Point was also of immediate concern for Ewell. His pleas for troops from Richmond finally paid dividends when Second Company, Richmond Howitzers, commanded by Lieutenant John Thompson Brown, arrived at Gloucester Point aboard the steamer *Logan* on 7 May 1861. Work had already commenced rebuilding the colonial-era fortifications, and the howitzers added their two guns, two Dahlgren boat howitzers, to the two old iron six-pounders that had been brought down from Gloucester C.H. The Howitzers had not positioned themselves too soon, as a Union gunboat, the USS *Yankee*, came within range, and a shell was sent whizzing toward the vessel. It was the first shot fired during the war in Virginia. Approximately fifteen rounds were fired at the *Yankee*, which returned two shells toward Gloucester Point. No damage was done by this exchange, and the *Yankee* soon withdrew from the York River. It was a glorious moment for the Richmond Howitzers. "All of our men were perfectly cool &

collected during the whole of the firing," Private James Williams recounted, "and Lieutenant Brown said we acted gallantly. I glory in the first shot in Virginia fired by the Howitzers and I helped to fire it."[3]

Coastal defense everywhere in Hampton Roads was a tremendous concern for the Confederates. Flag Officer French Forrest, known as a "blusterer of the real old-tar school"[4] and a hero of the Mexican War, was named commandant of the Gosport Navy Yard. Forrest immediately began reorganizing the yard and recognized the need to defend the Elizabeth River against any Federal naval operation. Forrest turned to the noted engineer Major General Walter Gwynn to create a defensive network. Gwynn, an 1822 United States Military Academy graduate, was an internationally esteemed railroad engineer and was considered the founder of the southeastern railroad network. When the war erupted, Gwynn joined the South Carolina militia and constructed batteries in Charleston Harbor facing Fort Sumter. When Fort Sumter surrendered, Gwynn was named major general of the Virginia Militia and sent to Norfolk. He participated in the capture of Gosport Navy Yard and then began constructing batteries at the mouth of the Elizabeth River. Eventually, 196 of the heavy cannon captured at Gosport would be used by Gwynn to build the strategic batteries at Sewell's Point, Craney Island and Pig Point.

Gwynn realized that Union control of Fort Monroe had given the Federals an advantage in Hampton Roads. He urged that more cannon and men be made available to fortify Hampton and other nearby points to prevent a Union blockade of Virginia's bays and rivers. As he supervised the work at Sewell's Point, General Gwynn watched the Federal steamers enter the Chesapeake Bay, bringing supplies and troops to either Fort Monroe or Washington, D.C. He also noticed how the Union naval squadron continued to increase its power. Gwynn and Flag Officer Austin Pendergrast of the USS *Cumberland* corresponded about the capture of Virginia merchant ships. Pendergrast reminded Gwynn it was war and the Federals took advantage of their naval superiority to control the shipping lanes. In Gwynn's mind, all of Virginia was at risk unless the growing Federal power was somehow curtailed.

More action was needed by the Confederates. Even though batteries were under construction, there were not enough men, particularly on the Peninsula, to guard against the Union troop buildup on Fort Monroe and the arrival of additional Union warships. The Reverend William Nelson

Pendleton, an 1830 West Point graduate, wrote Confederate President Jefferson Davis:

> *As you value our great cause, hasten on to Richmond. Lincoln and Scott are, if I mistake not, considering other demonstrations the great movement upon Richmond. Suppose they should send suddenly up the York River, as they can, an army of thirty thousand or more; these are no means at hand to repel them, and if their policy shown in Maryland gets footing here, it will be a severe, if not fatal blow.*[5]

Ewell was doing all he could to organize the Lower Peninsula. Since the arrival of additional troops on Fort Monroe, the citizens of Hampton had organized an informal patrol. The picket post at Mill Creek Bridge, which guarded the primary path to Fort Monroe, posted a Confederate flag.

Whether or not this flag was a provocation, Dimick decided he needed to occupy a portion of Elizabeth City County. On 13 May, his command was reinforced with 778 officers and men of the 1st Vermont Regiment, commanded by Colonel John Wolcott Phelps, and two additional companies of the 3rd Massachusetts, totaling 132 officers and men. Consequently, Dimick needed to secure a better water supply for all of these soldiers and

Mill Creek Bridge, 1861. *Courtesy of The Casemate Museum.*

advised Colonel Charles King Mallory, a Hampton lawyer and commander of the 115th Virginia Militia Regiment, that he intended to take possession of wells on the Elizabeth City County side of Mill Creek. That afternoon, Dimick led elements of the 4th Massachusetts and occupied the Mill Creek Bridge, as well as the Clark and Segar farms. Local volunteers serving as pickets were outraged by the Union advance and swore "vengeance on Massachusetts troops for the Invasion of Virginia." One cavalry vidette, Dr. William R. Vaughan, confronted Dimick and demanded, "By what right, sir, does your army cross that bridge and invade the sacred soil of Virginia?" Dimick reportedly snapped, "By God, sir, might makes right."[6]

Mallory was shocked by the Union action and called the local militia into service. Ewell, who had been promoted to lieutenant colonel and placed in command of the entire Lower Peninsula on 11 May, rushed to Hampton. On 14 May, Ewell secured an interview with Colonel Dimick to ascertain the Union commander's intentions. Dimick advised Ewell that he only needed the wells for the health of his troops. Ewell inquired if the Federals had any other plans to move against Hampton. Ewell noted Dimick's reply: "He laughed at the idea of violence being contemplated toward Hampton. He expressed great regret at the present state of things, and was kind and conciliatory."[7]

The Federals used this first occupied piece of Virginia soil to establish Camp Hamilton. Originally known as Camp Troy, the camp was renamed in honor of Lieutenant Colonel Schuyler Hamilton, Winfield Scott's military secretary. The 1st Vermont and 2nd New York were billeted at Camp Hamilton. The camp primarily consisted of tents and other temporary structures laid out in company streets. Due to the protection provided by the guns of Fort Monroe, little effort was made to provide the camp with extensive fortifications. Many soldiers moved beyond the confines of the camp. Massachusetts troops even converted former President John Tyler's home, Villa Margaret, into barracks. Tyler's wife, Julia, strove to rid her home of these "scum of the earth." She asked Northern authorities to protect her property, but to no avail.

Ewell was disturbed by the Union expansion; nevertheless, he recognized there was little he could do to stop the Federals. He met with Major John Baytop Cary on 14 May to quicken the organization of volunteers in Hampton and Elizabeth City County. Cary, an 1839 graduate of the College

Camp Hamilton, 1861. *Courtesy of The Casemate Museum.*

Colonel Benjamin
Stoddert Ewell, 1860.
*Courtesy of The Museum
of the Confederacy.*

of William and Mary and headmaster of the Hampton Military Academy, was ordered to establish a camp of construction for 820 men. Unfortunately, there were only three hundred muskets available, half of them obsolete flintlocks. Ewell also ordered Cary to keep his men over half a mile away from the Union lines to avoid any incidents.

The Federals continued to probe the Confederate defenses. Walter Gwynn was still in the process of arming the Sewell's Point Battery on 18 May when two Union gunboats, *Monticello* and *Thomas Freeborn*, shelled the Confederate position. When the Federals retired, Gwynn rushed Captain Peyton Colquitt's Columbus Lifeguards from Georgia into action, mounting thirty-two-pounders in the unfinished battery. The Federal gunboats returned the next day; however, they were greeted with return fire and driven off.

A little over a month had passed since Virginia's secession, and the Federals appeared determined to expand their position in Hampton Roads. Union gunboats enabled Fort Monroe to be resupplied at will, and the ever-increasing Federal troop strength placed the Federals in a position to begin a concerted effort to use the Peninsula as an avenue of advance against Richmond.

Chapter 2

Where Two Opposing
Forces Meet

As the first month of the war's drama on the Peninsula closed, the stage required new leaders of a different ilk. Onto the stage would now step two individuals who would dominate the Peninsula's military scene during the long, hot months of summer. These grand actors, one an experienced, professional soldier and the other a highly skilled politician, would transform the Civil War from a war of words and passion into a conflict of combat and casualties. Both men were flamboyant and ambitious and would leave a lasting mark on the Peninsula.

Winfield Scott recognized Fort Monroe as key to his policy to bring his native state of Virginia back into the Union. The reinforcements he had already sent and the additional troops he intended to transfer to the Peninsula necessitated, he believed, a change in command. He needed a higher-ranking officer to command the growing number of soldiers on Old Point Comfort. Scott wanted an aggressive leader who would actively contest Confederate positions threatening the Hampton Roads anchorage as well as secure the Peninsula as an avenue of approach against Richmond. Scott's selection was somewhat of a surprise. Instead of ordering a veteran officer to this critical post, he chose a politician turned militia officer, Major General Benjamin "Ben" Franklin Butler.

Ben Butler, an unlikely candidate for this position, first considered the command a demotion. Yet it placed him at the very center of events then unfolding in Virginia, a perfect platform for his ambition. Neither his visage nor his previous career indicated any martial aptitude or ardor. Nevertheless, Butler had already risen to hero status and was the first officer promoted by Lincoln to the rank of major general. A mercurial man who had already defied powerful politicians and seasoned generals during the war's first weeks, he was now poised to gain everlasting fame by capturing Richmond. On 21 May 1861, as he stepped onto Fort Monroe's Engineer's Wharf, Butler saw the opportunities that lay before him.

Born in Deerfield, New Hampshire, on 5 November 1818, Benjamin Franklin Butler was the son of the War of 1812 militia dragoon officer and privateer Captain John Butler. His father died while serving as a privateer in the Caribbean under a quasi-legal letter of marque, authorized by revolutionary Simon Bolivar. His impoverished widow, Charlotte Ellison Butler, eventually moved to Lowell, Massachusetts, to operate a respectable boardinghouse for millworkers. Young Ben, a somewhat frail child with a cast in one eye, immersed himself in books. He proved to be a good student while attending schools, including Exeter and Lowell. Family finances being limited, Butler worked briefly at Meachum and Mathewson's, a Lowell bookstore. He had hoped to follow in the footsteps of his martial ancestors (both grandfathers served during the Revolutionary War, and one, Zephaniah Butler, fought with Major General James Wolfe at Quebec) by seeking an appointment to West Point. The education would be free; but he would deeply disappoint his mother by not becoming a clergyman. However, no appointments were available. Rejected by West Point, Butler attended Waterville College, formerly known as the Maine Literary and Theological Institution and later as Colby College. As Butler's sharp, probing mind was out of place in this Baptist school, he decided to become a lawyer. Upon graduation in 1838 and following a four-month "toughening up" sea voyage with an uncle, he read law in the office of the well-respected Lowell attorney William Smith. A one-year stint teaching at an academy in Dracut, Massachusetts, slowed his law studies. Nevertheless, he passed the bar exam in 1840 after two years of study and promptly established his own practice in Lowell.

Butler "almost from the first acquired a marked reputation as a bold, astute, and not too scrupulous practitioner"[1] of the law. He first gained notoriety as a friend of the working class, defending young factory girls in their grievances with the textile mills that dominated Lowell's economy. In one case, Butler, looking for corporate property equal to the sum, attached a claim against a mill's water wheel; thus, the factory could not function without approval of the court. The claim was quickly settled in favor of the young girl.

Ben Butler became known as a "sharpster" for his clever maneuvering of the law. "I do not mean it should be understood that I win in all the sharp points I took; far from it," Butler reflected, "but I took them all the same and not infrequently won."[2] His legal work was epitomized by thorough preparation and debating skill. When cross-examining "experts," he strove to know as much as the eminent witnesses. Butler would challenge "hostile" physicians by asking such questions as, "Give me a list of names and the positions of all of the bones in the body."[3] When warned to be respectful to a Harvard professor, Butler retorted, "I am well aware of that. We hung one of them the other day."[4] Butler would learn anything, even how to drive a locomotive, if it would benefit his case. He would twist a case, based on his thorough knowledge of the law, to gain an acquittal. One judge, J.G. Abbott, declared that "in one faculty Butler was never excelled, that was the keeping out and getting in of evidence."[5]

As his fame spread, Butler expanded his client base and opened an office in Boston. J.Q.A. Griffin described him as the "most skilled lawyer, in many respects, now living in New England."[6] Accordingly, other opportunities besides criminal cases came his way because of his notoriety and skill. He prepared the specifications for Elias Howe's sewing machine patent. The documents were so well written that Singer Sewing Machine Company was eventually forced to pay Howe royalties for an infringement on his patented design. Butler was admitted to practice before the U.S. Supreme Court in 1845. He was only twenty-seven years old, and it is generally acknowledged that he was the youngest person to attain this honor. He handled personal litigation for President Franklin Pierce and represented John Sutter, on whose land the California gold rush began, in a case to reclaim Sutter's lost property. Amidst the confusion of Mexican land grants, the Treaty of Guadalupe Hidalgo, property rights and United States law, Butler succeeded in obtaining another land grant for Sutter. Even though Butler was often called a "notorious demagogue…so groveling and obscene,"[7] he had quickly become one of the most distinguished lawyers in America.

The wealth gained from his legal success prompted Butler to seek the hand of the beautiful, elegant and talented Sarah Hildreth. Daughter of

Benjamin Franklin Butler, portrayed in political cartoon by Thomas Nast, circa 1875. *Courtesy of The Casemate Museum.*

an affluent physician and sister of his close friend Fisher Ames Hildreth, Sarah was an accomplished professional actress who had won critical and popular acclaim. Sarah and Ben were married on 16 May 1844 and moved into a grand house, Belvidere, overlooking the Merrimac River in Lowell. Their union produced three children surviving infancy: Blanche (1847), Paul (1854) and Ben Israel (1856).

Butler's sharp mind, oratory skills and burning ambition led him to enter politics. Although the conservative forces of Whiggery dominated mainstream Massachusetts politics, Butler joined the Democratic Party. His first foray into turbulent politics as an advocate for Martin Van Buren during the 1840 election ended in failure. Butler was determined to rise above this setback and sought a cause he could call his own. He became a champion of the ten-hour workday. As with his representation of working girls in disputes with factory owners, Butler gained even greater notoriety for himself. Overnight, he became known as a friend of the working class and an avowed enemy of the Whig Party, which was dominated by factory owners. The ten-hour workday became a volatile political issue, dominating local elections. When factory owners sought to control the votes of their employees, Butler retorted, "We will vote as free men not as slaves."[8] Vicious editorials in Whig newspapers prompted Butler to sue one editor for criminal libel. Butler won his case, but a pro-Whig judge who considered Ben Butler little more than a "political scoundrel" quickly overturned it.[9] Nevertheless, the Massachusetts legislature eventually changed the law from a thirteen-hour workday to one that did not exceed eleven hours and fifteen minutes. It was a compromise victory. By then, Butler had purchased his own factory, Lowell's Middlesex Mill, and established a policy of a ten-hour workday. Butler's politics were his principles in action.

Butler became a "Barn-burner" within the Democratic Party during the 1850s. Despite his support for the Compromise of 1850 and the Fugitive Slave Law, Butler was able to forge a coalition of Democrats and Free Soilers to break the Whigs' hold over Massachusetts politics through skillful election maneuvering. Consequently, he was elected to the Massachusetts House of Representatives in 1852 and, six years later, to the State Senate. His power within the Democratic Party continued to grow. Butler gained the considerable voting support of Catholic Democrats when he supported a bill to rebuild Lowell's Ursuline Convent, which had been burned during an anti-Catholic riot sparked by Know-Nothings. He also sponsored legislation that established the Massachusetts Supreme Court in 1859.

Success in business, family and politics soothed only part of Butler's burning ambition. He dreamed of being a soldier, to attain the martial acclaim achieved by his ancestors. Rebuffed by West Point, he sought the only other avenue of military service available to an aspiring lawyer—the local militia. In 1839, Butler enrolled as a private in a newly formed Lowell militia company. He attended every drill and muster, which eventually led to his election as colonel of the 5th Massachusetts. Although he lost his command due to political action, he was elected brigadier general in 1857. As a Massachusetts militia brigade commander, he led his troops on an annual encampment.

Butler's prominence in Massachusetts Democratic politics placed him at center stage during the 1860 election crisis. He had attended every Democratic convention since 1848 and was very vocal in his defense of slavery. He believed that the Southern states had the constitutional right to practice slavery within their borders. Regardless of Butler's personal acceptance of this constitutional right, by 1860, his party was split over the issue of expanding slavery into the western territories. Despite his pledge as a Massachusetts delegate to support Stephen Douglas's candidacy, Butler sought to nominate a compromise candidate, such as James Guthrie of Kentucky, during the Charleston Democratic National Convention. Butler believed that only an "appeasement" candidate could keep the Democratic Party unified to win the presidential election.

Ben Butler voted seven times for Douglas and then switched his vote for Jefferson Davis of Mississippi. He voted fifty-seven consecutive times for the nomination of Davis. The convention eventually fell apart over the party platform, and Butler moved on to a reconvened convention in Baltimore. There, he supported Vice President John Cabell Breckenridge. When the party disintegrated, Butler continued to advocate Breckenridge and the Southern Democrats.

His pro-Southern stance made Butler unpopular back home in Massachusetts. Many Northern Democrats believed his actions "served to strengthen Southern extremists."[10] The "Breckenridge Democrats" in Massachusetts nominated Butler to run for governor, but he polled fewer than six thousand votes and was defeated.

The November 1860 election placed Abraham Lincoln in the White House and put in motion the secession of the Deep South states. Although President James Buchanan intended to do nothing about the crisis in his last months in office, Butler knew that secession meant war. Butler believed that the North would fight to preserve the Union, and he intended to play a leadership role during the conflict. Although he may have supported the constitutional right for Southern states to practice slavery, he could not condone secession and was prepared to evoke any force necessary to suppress what he considered rebellion.

Butler was in court when he learned that Secretary of War Simon Cameron had requested 1,500 Massachusetts militiamen from Governor John A. Andrews on 15 April 1861. The military-minded lawyer immediately walked out of court and began to command the brigade detailed to defend Washington, D.C. Not satisfied with his own communications with Simon Cameron requesting this appointment, Butler went to a Boston bank and secured a loan to underwrite militia transportation only if he were named brigade commander. Meanwhile, Butler became a war profiteer by procuring a contract for his mill to provide wool for soldiers' overcoats.

When Butler went to Governor Andrews seeking the command, Andrews rejected his offer, stating that his political crony, Brigadier General Ebenezer Peirce, was the more senior officer. Accordingly, Peirce should assume the mantle of leadership. Andrews soon learned that Butler had hoodwinked him. Without ready cash in the state budget to send the militia south, only a loan would enable Massachusetts to fulfill its troop commitment. The bank's position: no Butler, no loan. Thus, Brigadier General Benjamin Franklin Butler, Esquire, assumed command of the first Massachusetts troops to entrain southward.

Butler's appointment met with a score of varying opinions. Several seasoned soldiers questioned his lack of military experience. The Republican administration, however, was overjoyed by Butler's conversion to the cause. As an outspoken Democrat previously in favor of states' rights, "Butler," as Wendall Phillips remarked, "and a score of such Democrats, by accepting commissions, and flinging their fortunes with the flag, settled the doubt (as to a war of one party), and saved the Union."[11] Butler believed that he was as experienced and capable as Winfield Scott and enjoyed the crowds that cheered on the Massachusetts militiamen as they moved on toward Washington. Filled with the glory of the march through New York City, Butler was reminded by Senator Edward Dickinson Baker, "All very well, General; for them to cheer you when they go out, but take care of them so that they will cheer you on their return."[12]

As Butler's main body of troops reached Philadelphia, the general learned that his advance guard, the 6th Massachusetts, had been attacked by a violent, pro-secessionist mob in Baltimore on 19 April 1861. Three Massachusetts militiamen were killed and thirty-six wounded. It was the first bloodshed of the war. Of even greater impact upon Butler's plans was

Major General Benjamin Franklin Butler. *Courtesy of The Casemate Museum.*

that pro-Confederate Marylanders had cut communications between the North and Washington. Led by West Point graduate and railroad engineer Isaac Trimble, Maryland secessionists burned the railroad bridges and cut the telegraph lines leading north from Baltimore. Washington was isolated, Baltimore was seething and Butler's path to the capital appeared blocked.

Ben Butler was not to be denied his chance for glory as the savior of Washington and sought an alternative route. He met with Captain Samuel Francis DuPont, commandant of the Philadelphia Navy Yard, who suggested that Butler use the Chesapeake Bay. If the pro-Southern town of Annapolis could be secured, then troublesome Baltimore would be bypassed via the Elk Ridge and Baltimore & Ohio Railroad.

On 20 April 1861, the 8th Massachusetts moved to Perryville, Maryland, via the Philadelphia, Wilmington & Baltimore Railroad. At Perryville, the railroad operated a ferry service, situated where the Susquehanna River empties into the Chesapeake Bay. Butler obtained the use of the ferryboat *Maryland*, embarked his troops and steamed down the bay to Annapolis.

If Baltimore was considered dangerous for Unionists, Annapolis was treacherous. Secessionists were hatching plots to occupy the U.S. Naval Academy and the USF *Constitution*, which was then in use as a training ship. When the *Maryland* chugged into Annapolis Harbor late in the evening of 20 April, Lieutenant George Rogers sounded general quarters on the *Constitution* and prepared to fire four thirty-two-pounder stern guns at the approaching steamer. Rogers hailed the vessel, and to his relief, it was filled with Ben Butler and 724 Massachusetts militiamen. Since the venerable warship was grounded at its moorings off the academy, Butler ordered the *Maryland* to tow "Old Ironsides" out into the Severn River. This action prompted many Butler detractors back in Boston to exclaim humorously, "Butler saves the 'Constitution.'"[13]

The 8th Massachusetts was soon joined by the 7th New York, which arrived on 22 April 1861, via the Chesapeake Capes. Commanded by Colonel Marshall Leffrets, the 7th New York was an elite volunteer unit filled with prominent New Yorkers. When Butler tried to assume command of the 7th since he was the highest-ranking officer, Leffrets rejected his claim. A West Pointer on his staff advised Leffrets that a militia commander from one state could not command another state's militia regardless of rank. Butler was incensed and wrote, "That was the first time in carrying on the war that West Point had ever interfered to render my movements abortive, but not the last time by a good deal…It stirred me then, as it always had stirred me since."[14]

Regardless, Butler took command, and despite the protests of Governor Thomas Hicks of Maryland, the Union troops occupied Annapolis. The pro-Southern town treated the militiamen with scorn. Businesses closed their doors to Northern soldiers, and secessionists damaged railroad equipment. The tracks connecting Annapolis with the B&O were breached at several locations. Butler, operating without orders, was nevertheless determined to break the "Siege of Washington." Locomotives were repaired, and work gangs organized to rebuild tracks. Soon a train was operating, defended by a howitzer mounted on a flat car. Butler had overawed the secessionist firebrands, and on 25 April 1861, the 7th New York entered Washington.

Butler was quickly rewarded for his resolute actions saving the capital. A new military district, Department of Annapolis, was established on 27 April 1861. It encompassed twenty miles on either side of the railroad leading from Annapolis to Washington. Of course, Butler was named department commander. He was overjoyed with his appointment, as he believed that it vindicated the role of the militia during the crisis. "A high honor never yet conferred upon a military general who had seen no service,"[15] he wrote his wife. The Massachusetts politician and weekend soldier was now a hero and sought to gain even greater fame.

The department's headquarters was established just nine miles from Baltimore at the Relay House in Annapolis Junction. There Butler could keep an eye on the rebellious city. "Mobtown," as the city was often called, was still seething with secession. Indeed, all of Maryland was in an uproar over the movement of Union troops within the state. Governor Hicks moved the legislature's special session considering secession to Frederick. While the Marylanders chastised the Federal government for forcing war upon the Southern states, cooler heads prevailed, and Maryland proclaimed itself neutral. Despite this decision, Federal policy was crafted to limit any aggressive actions toward Maryland yet still enable the Unionists to occupy and use Maryland's transportation systems.

Butler, however, refused to sit idly at Annapolis Junction. He learned that Baltimore secessionists were still organizing and collecting arms. He, therefore, sent his own special agent, Captain Peter Haggerty, dressed as an organ grinder (including a monkey), to glean information. Haggerty soon reported that regardless of pro-Southern rhetoric, Baltimore could be occupied by Union troops without bloodshed at any time.

Meanwhile, Winfield Scott had issued ambiguous commands for Butler to stop Maryland Confederates from gathering war material in Baltimore. Scott, however, did not give direct orders to occupy the troublesome city. Instead, the old hero developed his own ponderous plan, whereby four columns of three thousand men each would converge upon Baltimore from all directions. Butler fumed at Scott, known as "Old Fuss and Feathers." The Department of Annapolis commander believed that the time for action was at hand and concocted a plan to open the door to Baltimore.

On 13 May, Butler loaded one thousand soldiers aboard a train headed toward Harpers Ferry. As Confederate spies rode off to Baltimore to alert fellow secessionists of this movement, Butler cut the telegraph lines. The troops had traveled two miles westward when the train was stopped and reversed to Baltimore. Butler's task force, including elements of the 6th

Massachusetts, arrived in Baltimore after dark during a violent rainstorm. Lightning illuminated the drenched soldiers as they marched from Camden Yards to Federal Hill. Once atop the promontory that commanded the city and harbor, Butler sent word to the Federal garrison at Fort McHenry that the Union had taken possession of Baltimore. The next morning, Butler issued a proclamation stating the rules and regulations he intended to enforce. The Baltimoreans did not murmur a word in opposition. Mobtown was completely subdued by Butler's occupation.

Butler also sent a small force to Frederick, where they arrested multimillionaire secessionist Ross Winans. Winans, a noted inventor who was manufacturing weapons for the Confederacy, was accused of treason and imprisoned. Butler intended to make an example of Winans. He "thought that if such a man, worth $15,000,000, were hanged for treason, it would convince the people of Maryland, at least that we were upon no picnic."[16] The Union general never had the opportunity to hang Winans in Union Square, as circumstances and his position would quickly change.

Ben Butler was lauded throughout the North for his determined service ending Maryland's secessionist movement. General in Chief Winfield Scott, in turn, was enraged. On 16 May, he sent a chiding telegram to Butler: "Sir: Your hazardous occupation of Baltimore was made without my knowledge, and of course, without my approbation. It is a godsend that it is without conflict of arms. It is also reported that you have sent a detachment to Frederick; but this is impossible. Not a word have I received from as to either movement. Let me hear from you."[17]

He did not reply, prompting Scott to send another message ordering Butler to "issue no more proclamations."[18] Butler knew that Scott's displeasure meant that he would soon be relieved of his command. Despite Scott's censure, Butler received a telegram that evening from President Lincoln appointing him major general. The next day, Major General George Cadwalader took over command from Butler at Baltimore, with orders for Butler to report to Fort Monroe, Virginia, and "assume command of the post."[19]

Instead, Butler went to Washington to pick up his commission in person. There he met with President Lincoln, stating that he was unsure he should accept his promotion. Butler believed that his new assignment was a reproof for his actions in Maryland. He refused such a demotion and threatened to return home and resume his law practice. Lincoln and other cabinet members assured Butler that his new duties included command of territory in a sixty-mile radius around Fort Monroe. Butler met with Winfield Scott the next morning. Scott confirmed Butler's new appointment as commander of the Union Department of Virginia and North Carolina.

During the war's first month, Butler had created a sensation. Torchlit parades were held in his honor throughout the North. Despite his disagreement with Winfield Scott, President Lincoln needed Butler. His Democratic Party affiliations were desperately required by the Republican administration to broaden public support for the war. Yet he did not look the part of a general. A British journalist described Butler as "a stout, middle-aged man, strongly built, with coarse limbs, his features indicative of great shrewdness and craft, his forehead high, the elevation being of some degree due perhaps to the want of hair, with a strong obliquity of vision, which may perhaps have been caused by an injury as the eyelid hangs with a pendulous droop over the organ."[20]

Major General Benjamin Franklin Butler. *Courtesy of The Casemate Museum.*

Another observer described Butler after his triumphal entrance into Baltimore:

> *I found him clothed in a gorgeous military uniform adorned with rich gold embroidery. His rotund form, his squinting eye, and the peculiar puff of his cheeks made him look a little grotesque. Only a person much more devoid of a sense of humor than I was, would have failed to notice that General Butler thoroughly enjoyed his position of power, which of course, was new to him, and that he keenly appreciated its theatrical possibilities…while we were conversing, officers entered from time to time to make reports or to ask for orders. Nothing could have been more striking than the air of authority with which the General received them, and the tone of court premptoriousness peculiar to the military commander on the stage, with which he expressed his satisfaction or discontent, and with which he gave his instructions. And, after every such scene, he looked around with a sort of triumphant gaze, as if to assure himself that the bystanders were duly impressed.[21]*

The evening of 21 May 1861, Butler was en route to Fort Monroe aboard the Old Bay Line steamer *Adelaide*. At the same time, the Confederates were seeking a new commander for the Peninsula. Even though Major

Fortress Monroe, 1859. *Courtesy of The Casemate Museum.*

Benjamin Stoddert Ewell had achieved everything feasible to muster and organize volunteers on the Peninsula, much more was required. The majority of Ewell's volunteers were still poorly trained and equipped. Ewell, operating without an adequate staff, continually rushed from Williamsburg to Yorktown or Hampton striving to resolve problems and seek more men. While reinforcements had arrived in the guise of Montague's Battalion from King and Queen County, the unit was not directly under Ewell's control and was stationed at Yorktown. More importantly, the beleaguered Ewell was unable to begin work on a defensive line below Williamsburg designed to block any Federal advance.

Robert E. Lee, then commander of the Provisional Army of Virginia, realized that the rapidly increasing Union forces at Fort Monroe posed an immediate threat to Richmond. Consequently, Lee detailed Colonel John Bankhead Magruder on 21 May 1861 to assume "command of the troops and military operations on the line to Hampton." Magruder was instructed to establish his headquarters at Yorktown and "take measures for the safety of the batteries at Jamestown Island and York River, and urge forward the construction of the defenses between College and Queen Creeks in advance of Williamsburg."[22]

"Prince John," as he was known by many of his old army acquaintances from his stylish dress, courtly manners, lavish entertainments and amateur theatrics, was born in Villeboro near Port Royal, Virginia, on 1 May 1807. One of eight children, John was the son of Thomas and Elizabeth Bankhead Magruder. Thomas was a successful attorney in Caroline County. John, along with his brother Allan, attended Rappahannock Academy near Moss Neck Plantation. On 6 September 1825, John attended the University of Virginia's start-up session. He was one of 123 students.

Shortly after his arrival in Charlottesville, Magruder became involved in a "student rebellion" on 1 October 1825. Thomas Jefferson, the university's creator, had sought to bring together some of Europe's most distinguished professors. Several students protested the "harsh regimen of these" foreign professors, particularly George Long and Thomas Newett Key. On the evening of 30 September, a bottle filled with a vile substance was thrown through a window at Professor Long. The next evening a group of students, disguised with masks, gathered on the lawn and demonstrated. Professors Emmet and Tucker strove to quell the disruption by attacking the ringleader.

The situation evolved into a riot, yet somehow the professors escaped from the mob. The next day, sixty-five students, including Magruder, signed a petition criticizing the actions of Emmet and Tucker.

Jefferson considered the affair one of the saddest of his life and took swift disciplinary action. Magruder was certainly at the scene; however, he had not participated in the demonstration. Even though three student "ringleaders" were expelled, Magruder was reprimanded for signing the remonstrance against the professors.

Nevertheless, Magruder proved to be a good student. He excelled in mathematics and studied "Ancient Languages." His tenure at the university brought him into contact with several outstanding individuals, including William Ballard Preston, Philip St. George Cocke and Edgar Allan Poe. Magruder's time in Charlottesville also enabled him to meet Thomas Jefferson, who visited the campus almost daily until his death in 1826.

Magruder also left the university in 1826. He had received an appointment from Congressman R.S. Garnett to the United States Military Academy at West Point. His roommates, all destined to become Confederate officers, were William Nelson Pendleton, Lloyd J. Beall and William Cruger Heywood.

Cadet Magruder performed rather well at West Point. Despite his demerits (totaling 196 one year), Magruder rose to the rank of sergeant of First Company in his third year and was elevated to captain of First Company during the 1829–30 school year. He also served as a member, along with Jefferson Davis, in the "Hose Company." The first squad, commanded by Lieutenant John H. Winder, featured a small fire engine. These activities did not disrupt Magruder's academic work. He ranked fifteenth in his class upon graduation.

The personality traits that would define Magruder became evident at West Point. An unidentified correspondent for the *Army and Navy Journal* wrote that Magruder "was perhaps the most elegant and *distingue* cadet at the academy in those days, and I do not believe West Point had ever had his equal. He was a first-rate soldier, of fine appearance and very strict when on duty as 'officer of the day,' never failing to report the slightest violations of the regulations, even though the delinquent was his most intimate friend and room-mate… John was for the corps the orbiter of things elegant, the glass of fashion."[23] By the end of his West Point career, Magruder had become a "polished and popular society man,"[24] reflected Benjamin Stoddert Ewell.

Major General John Bankhead Magruder, 1860. *Courtesy of Virginia War Museum.*

The fun-loving side of John Magruder resulted in several incidents and numerous demerits. "Magruder like Pendleton," wrote Pendleton's daughter, "was something of a musician, playing on the flute, and the two enjoyed their music so much that their room was not infrequently reported for 'music in study hours.'"[25] Drinking also began plaguing Magruder's life while at West Point. He was involved in the famous "Eggnog Riots" of 1826. Magruder and several other cadets, including Jefferson Davis, were apprehended consuming "spirituous liquor." When ordered to their rooms, Magruder and many other revelers did so. Several other intoxicated cadets, however, proceeded to use "clubs and other weapons to drive the officers out of the barracks or into their own quarters."[26] While thirty-nine cadets were expelled, Magruder escaped punishment.

When Magruder graduated in 1830, he was posted to the Seventh Infantry. He did not report. Instead, Magruder requested a yearlong furlough due to illness. During the year, Magruder lobbied a transfer to the Topographical Engineers or Artillery. Through the intercession of his uncle, Colonel James

Bankhead, he was eventually assigned to the First Artillery. He also took the time while on extended leave to get married.

On 18 May 1831, John Bankhead Magruder married the wealthy Baltimore heiress Henrietta Von Kapff. Even though three children—Isabell (1833), Kate (1835) and Henry (1838)—were produced by the Magruders, the union was not perfect. Lieutenant Magruder "appeared to only have two objects in view—one to make a great show and the other to have a good time in society."[27] His carefree spending, heavy drinking, flirtation and other dissipations sorely strained their marriage. "His wife was a very weak, but a good woman, and in love with him to an uncommon degree," John Fitzgerald Lee reflected. "But he managed to alienate her devoted attachment, to make her separate from him and leave him to the irregular life which was anything but happy or respectable."[28] Henrietta Magruder eventually left her husband and moved to Italy during the early 1840s.

In October 1832, Magruder reported for his first duty assignment as Fort McHenry's recruiting officer. He was ordered to Fort Macon near Beaufort, North Carolina, in February 1835 and then to Fort Johnson outside Wilmington, North Carolina, in August. While serving in North Carolina, Magruder studied law and was admitted to the North Carolina bar.

Lieutenant J.B. Magruder was temporarily placed in command of Fort Washington on the Potomac River but was soon thereafter transferred to the Topographical Bureau in Washington, D.C. Magruder had long coveted this assignment; however, due to the army's need for more men to fight the Seminoles in Florida, he did not enjoy his position long. He was ordered south to join his regiment and served with Company I during Brigadier General S. Jessup's 1837–38 winter campaign. The First Artillery was to subdue the Cherokees along the North Carolina–Tennessee border in April 1838, but after a few uneventful months, the unit was transferred to the Canadian border in September 1838. Magruder served at Plattsburg, New York, until March, when his unit was sent to Hancock Barracks in Houlton, Maine, to quell a border dispute, known as the Aroostook War.

This service along the Canadian border was tedious for Magruder. Opportunities for advancement and promotion seemed very remote. Magruder lobbied for a transfer and initiated his own campaign to gain a promotion. He had been a first lieutenant since 1836 and believed that he warranted advancement. Brigadier General William Jenkins Worth noted that Magruder "is now perhaps one of the oldest if not the oldest 1st lieutenant in the army and he is, by general agreement the most accomplished and soldierly man in the service by education, habits and association."[29] Magruder entreated his uncle, Colonel James Bankhead, for support. Bankhead, however, was somewhat displeased with his nephew's habits, as one observer noted:

> *But John's dissipations, debts, and escapades of various sorts, wearied the patience of his uncle, who one day took to lecturing his nephew for his conduct. Grasping a pinch of snuff, the old Colonel commenced with: John, why the devil can't you behave yourself? You are always in some damned scrape, and now these fellows are complaining that you won't pay their bills for champagne and cigars. Now there's your brother George…who is a quiet and well-behaved gentleman as ever lived; why is it that you are not like him.*[30]

Somewhat rebuffed by his uncle, Magruder sought medical assistance to secure a transfer. Two doctors concurred that he suffered from chronic bronchitis and suggested that he be assigned to a milder climate. In December 1844, Lieutenant Magruder was detailed to Oglethorpe Barracks in Savannah, Georgia.

Magruder was not destined to stay in Savannah long. Relations with Mexico had begun to sour over the United States' efforts to annex Texas. As the dispute increased in intensity, the United States began to prepare for war. Magruder rejoined Company B, First Artillery, in New York and sailed to Texas aboard the transport *Lexington*. His company arrived near Corpus Christi, Texas, on 4 October 1845 and was assigned to General Zachary Taylor's Army of Observation. Soon after his arrival, Magruder was requested to establish an eight-hundred-seat theater and manage its productions, thus keeping the troops "out of the gambling dens set up by camp followers." Shakespeare's *Othello*, featuring such young officers as James Longstreet and U.S. Grant, was but one of the plays performed.

Taylor, however, had little desire for his army to sit idle in camp. On 8 March 1846, he began his movement from the coastal camps toward the Rio Grande and the Mexican army. By May, Taylor was in position to fight in the battles of Palo Alto and Resaca de la Palma. Magruder and Company B did not play an active role in these battles. Nevertheless, the engagements gave Magruder the opportunity to observe light artillery, the so-called "flying batteries" units, in action. He immediately initiated a campaign to secure a transfer to one of these batteries.

In the midst of this active campaign, Magruder was reassigned to recruiting duty at Fort McHenry. While Magruder was in Baltimore, James Bankhead, who was a close friend of General in Chief Winfield Scott, actively lobbied for his nephew's advancement. Consequently, John Bankhead Magruder was detailed to command Company I, First Artillery, a light artillery unit, and was promoted to captain, effective 1 January 1847. Furthermore, Magruder was ordered to proceed with his command to Tampico, Mexico, as a part of Winfield Scott's expeditionary force. Magruder, after sixteen years of military service, had finally received his captaincy and, more importantly, the opportunity to become a grand actor on the stage of war.

Captain Magruder's company was assigned to David E. Twigg's division during the Siege of Vera Cruz. Once Vera Cruz fell, Scott sent his army toward Mexico City on the National Road. The Mexicans, led by General Antonio Lopez de Santa Anna, first attempted to block the Americans' march at Cerro Gordo. Magruder's light artillery was at the forefront of the action during the battle. "Captain Magruder's gallantry was conspicuously displayed on several occasions," reported brigade commander Colonel William S. Harney.[31] Magruder captured several enemy field guns and used them to pound the fleeing Mexicans. This "gallant and meritorious conduct" during the battle resulted in his promotion to brevet major. Reports of his dashing leadership spread throughout the army, prompting many, like the young Lieutenant Thomas J. Jackson, to comment, "I wanted to see active service, to be near the enemy and in the fight; and when I heard that John Magruder had his battery, I bent all of my energies to be with him, for I knew if any fighting was to be done, Magruder would be on hand."[32]

Company I was transferred to Brigadier General Gideon J. Pillow's division for the final advance on Mexico City. The difficult terrain forced Scott to send Pillow's command across the supposedly impassable Pedregal on a path discovered by Robert E. Lee. Magruder dragged his artillery across the lava field and, spearheading Pillow's advance, placed his guns in an exposed position to duel the Mexicans' heavy artillery near the village of Contreras. This action enabled the American infantry to prepare for their crushing victory on 20 August 1847.

After a brief armistice, Scott's army advanced on Mexico City's San Cosme and San Belen gates. Magruder played a minor role, defending the army's left flank during the fierce engagement at El Molina Del Ray. During the assault upon the fortress of Chapultepec, Magruder's artillery once again served on the army's left flank. Even though he was slightly wounded twice by grapeshot during the battle, his brilliant handling of light artillery batteries helped foil the Mexican attempt to repulse the American attack. The fall of Chapultepec basically ended the war and placed Magruder on center stage in a glorious fashion. Magruder was brevetted lieutenant colonel for his gallant actions and awarded a gold sword by the Commonwealth of Virginia. One of his soldiers, Corporal George Ballentine, called Magruder "a dashing officer...distinguished for his skill in light artillery maneuvers."[33]

These honors were indeed an appropriate tribute to John Bankhead Magruder, the so-called "El Capitan Colorado." Magruder, according to William Booth Taliaferro, had "gained that sobriquet from the flashy

Major General John Bankhead Magruder, 1860. *Courtesy of Virginia War Museum.*

uniform which he wore which rivaled that of Murat in the gold lace and red stripes with which it was decorated."[34] His flamboyant dress was noted by all. George Derby, a fellow officer, proposed a debate asking, "Are Magruder's pants blue with red stripes or red with blue stripes?" The joke concluded with the realization that Magruder's ornate, well-adorned uniform "exceeded even the generous limits of the regulations."[35]

Magruder did much to live up to the title "Prince John" while serving in occupied Mexico City. He became the toast of the town, reverting to his "gay, rollicking devil-may-care 'habits.'"[36] Alexander Watkins Terrell remembered that Magruder slapped the face of Brigadier General Franklin Pierce while playing cards. Prince John challenged the future president to a duel, which fortunately was never held. "Magruder was a bad example for young men to follow," wrote Captain Edward C. Boynton. "Ambitions, unscrupulous, treacherous, and dissolute," Boynton added, "he had one good quality at least—he was a dashing fearless soldier."[37]

Magruder was one of the founders of the socially elite Aztec Club in Mexico City. The prestigious club organized dinners and other entertainments for its members and guests. Prince John served as the Aztec Club's second vice-president until he left Mexico in November 1847 due to health problems.

Magruder returned to Baltimore, where he enjoyed a brief reunion with his family. He sought an appointment as commander of Fort McHenry. Magruder was rebuffed on this request as well as his plan to maintain Company I, First Artillery, as a mounted unit. Instead, he was ordered to take his unit to San Diego, California. Prince John reverted to his fun-loving ways while in California. Samuel Heintzelman recorded that "Colonel Magruder is having a nice time with his men. They are getting drunk."[38] Magruder became the toast of the town. He dabbled in real estate and "was given a dozen lots because of his charm."[39] Prince John owned and operated a saloon, the El Dorado, in Los Angeles, passed the California bar to practice law and was named president of the San Diego–based Atlantic & Pacific Railroad. He appears to have given little time to his military duties, rather spending hours, according to Samuel Heintzelman, "to enjoy the fleshpots of Los Angeles."[40] Magruder was only involved in one military action while in California, and his army accounts were audited twice for misuse of government property.

In 1853, Magruder returned to Washington, where he unsuccessfully lobbied to remount his artillery company. He also penned several articles on military and political affairs for various newspapers, such as the *Richmond Examiner*. Magruder requested an assignment to observe European armies. Instead, he was granted leave to visit his family in Italy. He arrived in Paris on 30 March 1854, just as the French were completing their preparations for the Crimean War. Magruder observed that French army in the field and reportedly "astonished the French officers by sleeping at the front with the Chasseurs under fire."[41] Magruder returned to the United States in the summer of 1855 with his wife and family; however, he was immediately ordered to join his unit in San Antonio, Texas.

Magruder served on the Texas frontier until 1856, when his company was ordered to Pentagon Barracks at Baton Rouge. He then was assigned to assume command of Fort Adams near Newport, Rhode Island. This assignment was perfect for Prince John. Newport, one of the most fashionable resorts in the nation, provided "a fine field for exercising his high social qualities and fondness for military display."[42] Armistead L. Long noted that Magruder's "princely hospitality and the brilliant show-drills with which he entertained his visitors made Fort Adams one of the most attractive features of the most celebrated watering place in America."[43]

The bon vivant Magruder was ordered in May 1859 to march his company overland to Fort Leavenworth, Kansas, where he was to assume command of the post. In addition to his garrison duties, Magruder took charge of the Artillery School of Practice. Several officers destined for fame studied at Leavenworth under Magruder's tutelage, including Armistead L. Long, Arnold Elzey, William H.F. "Rooney" Lee and Henry Jackson Hunt. "The aesthetical and precise Bankhead Magruder…was a good showman or ringmaster. He instituted pageants for our edification, sham battles and such like," wrote Artillery School student A.F. Callahan. "The artillery boomed over the prairies," Callahan added, "and reverberated through the fastness much to our amusement."[44] Armistead Long remembered:

> *Magruder brought with him the disposition that had characterized him at Newport. Although in the West the brilliant show-drills and dress-parades were often only witnessed by a group of frontiersman or a squad of Indians from the plains, he appeared as well satisfied as on similar occasions at Newport, where the spectators were the gay crowd of a fashionable watering-place.*[45]

Each of these grand parades concluded with a lavish dinner "provided with all the taste of a connoisseur," ended Long.[46]

In October 1860, Magruder was ordered to Washington, where he received a special assignment from Secretary of War John C. Floyd to study advances in European artillery. Magruder immediately went overseas. He spent some time with his family and observed the Sardinian army's Siege of Gaeta.

Prince John returned to Washington on 10 March 1861. There, he assumed command of Company I in defense of Washington. The fall of Fort Sumter placed Magruder, momentarily, in a difficult situation. In the days before Virginia left the Union, Prince John was called upon to escort President Abraham Lincoln in the capital city and met with him to discuss security matters. At that time, he confided to the president that he "very much regretted secession" but felt compelled to fight with "those

Major General John Bankhead Magruder. *Courtesy of Virginia War Museum.*

among whom I was born and bred, my relations, and friends all of whom believe they are right."[47] Magruder resigned his commission on 20 April 1861 and, with all the flourish of a grand knight on parade, proclaimed to Virginia's Governor's Advisory Council that "I have just crossed the Long Bridge, which is guarded by my old Battery. Give me 5,000 men and if I don't take Washington, you may take not only sword, but my life."[48] The council declined his rash advice to march against Washington and decided instead to use his talents to train the thousands of recruits descending upon Richmond. Commissioned a colonel in the Provisional Army of Virginia, he was detailed to organize an artillery training camp at the Richmond Baptist Seminary. Three weeks later, he was ordered to assume command on the Peninsula.

John Bankhead Magruder appeared to be the perfect choice for the Peninsula Command. The *San Antonio Light* reported:

> *Magruder was a wonderful man. He stood six feet four inches in height, and had a form that men envied and women adored. His nerves were all iron. Foreign travel and comprehensive culture had given him the zest that was always crisp and sparkling...he could fight all day and dance all night. In the morning a glass of brandy and a good cigar renewed his strength and caused the cup of his youth to run over with the precious wine of health and good spirits.[49]*

At fifty-one years of age and possessing a "certain aptitude for independent command,"[50] Magruder's flamboyant and seasoned leadership appeared to be the cure for the Peninsula's defensive needs.

Chapter 3

Battle Lines Are Drawn

General Butler received orders from Winfield Scott to cooperate with U.S. Naval forces to destroy any Confederate batteries erected at Craney Island and to recapture Gosport Navy Yard. Furthermore, Butler was to stop the Confederates from building any batteries that might threaten Fort Monroe and to capture any enemy positions that were within a half-day's march of the fort. Scott concluded his orders stating, "Boldness in execution is nearly always necessary, but in planning and fitting out expeditions or detachments great circumspection is a virtue. In important cases, where time clearly permits, be sure to submit your plans and ask instructions from higher authority."[1] Butler decided he would act immediately to expand the Union position on the Peninsula.

On 23 May 1861, Butler ordered Colonel John Wolcott Phelps to march the 1st Vermont into Hampton to disrupt the vote that was being taken to confirm Virginia's Ordinance of Secession. Phelps was a seasoned soldier. He had graduated from West Point in 1836 and was assigned to the 4th Artillery. He served with distinction in the Seminole and Mexican Wars. From 1856 to 1857, Phelps had served at Fort Monroe on a board establishing a system of artillery instruction. His final duty before resigning his commission in November 1859 was in Colonel Albert Sidney Johnston's Mormon Expedition. Phelps called the Mormons like "a snake coiled in the desert and concluded that it, like the snake, should be smitten."[2] Phelps had resigned "from conscientious scruples" arising from his dissatisfaction with the political power of the slave states. Once he returned to Vermont, he published numerous articles supporting the abolitionist cause and preservation of the Union.

The unit mustered at Rutland, Vermont, on 3 May 1861, and Phelps assumed command. Within three days, Phelps reported that the regiment was equipped and ready to march. On 8 May, the 1st Vermont received its colors from Governor Fairbanks. Fairbanks pointed to the single star as he gave the flag to Phelps:

> *In your hands, supported by these troops, I feel that this flag will never be dishonored, nor the State of Vermont disgraced. I charge you to remember that this flag represents but one star in that other flag, which I now present, bearing the national emblem, the stars and stripes. Vermont claims no separate nationality. Her citizens, ever loyal to the Union and Constitution, will rally in their strength for the preservation of the National Government and the honor of our country's flag.*[3]

The unit went by train to New York City; each man marched through the town wearing in his cap an evergreen sprig. The *New York Herald* commented: "To say that every man of the First Regiment of Vermont Light Infantry is the exact type of a soldier, is nothing more than is justly due them. They are slashing, dashing, brawny, well-knit fellows with deep determination stamped in every lineament of their countenances."[4] As the Vermonters marched down Broadway, Phelps rode at the head of the regiment, "tall and of massive form, with an immense Army hat and black ostrich plume." One bystander commented, "Who is that big Vermont Colonel?"[5] The response was quickly given: "Oh, that is old Ethan Allen resurrected!" The Vermonters then took the steamer *Alabama* south to Fort Monroe and were initially billeted in the Hygeia Hotel. They were soon reassigned to Camp Hamilton, where Phelps drilled the men and maintained them at a high readiness for active service.

The orders Phelps received from Butler entailed that he was just to march his command into Hampton, close the polls and then return to Camp Hamilton. Hampton was a town of almost 1,000 residents; however, the Confederates had not made any attempt to develop defenses because of the community's proximity to Fort Monroe. The town was defended by Cary's command of 130 poorly armed men, camped just outside the town. Cary already knew that the Federals would eventually march into Hampton and had made plans to burn the Hampton Creek Bridge to thwart any such movement. When Phelps's Vermonters approached Hampton on 23 May, Cary went into action. Unfortunately, he could locate neither the firing party nor the combustibles. Cary somehow was able to start a small fire, yet it was slow to set the span into flames. Phelps saw the wisps of smoke rise from the bridge and ordered his men to the double-quick to capture the bridge. As he noted the Vermonters' rapid approach, Cary sent one of his former teachers at Hampton Military Academy, VMI graduate Lieutenant Wilfred E. Cutshaw, to ascertain the Union's purpose. Cutshaw spurred his house through the flames across the bridge and met with Colonel Phelps. Phelps informed Cutshaw that his troops had no hostile intent "but simply…to reconnoiter."[6] With these assurances that neither the town nor its population would be molested, Cary and some citizens and the Vermonters joined together to extinguish the flames. Cary then moved his

"Edward"—student at Hampton Military Academy, 1860. *Courtesy of the Hampton History Museum.*

command out of Hampton. Phelps marched into the town, closed the polls and returned to Camp Hamilton. Once the Federals had left, Hampton residents immediately reopened the polls and overwhelmingly voted for secession. Phelps's "reconnoitering expedition" proved that the Union could march virtually at will wherever and whenever it wished throughout the Lower Peninsula. Ewell, recently promoted to lieutenant colonel, rushed that afternoon toward Fort Monroe to ascertain Butler's intentions. He was captured en route by Federal pickets. Major John Baytop Cary also traveled to Fort Monroe and secured Ewell's release.

While Hampton's white residents may have been in an uproar over this Union advance, local African Americans were overjoyed. This first encounter between bondsmen and Union soldiers prompted three slaves— Sheppard Mallory, Frank Baker and James Townsend, owned by Colonel Charles K. Mallory—to take "advantage of the terror prevailing among white inhabitants"[7] and escape into Union lines.

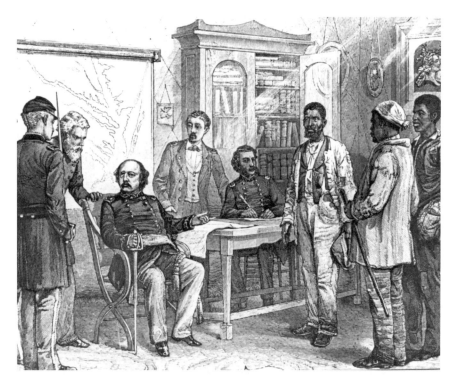

Contraband of war decision, 1861. *Courtesy of The Casemate Museum.*

Even before the Confederates learned of these runaway slaves, Cary went to Butler at Fort Monroe to learn "how far he intended to take possession of Virginia soil in order that I might act in such a manner as to avoid collision between our scouts."[8] Butler advised Cary that the Federals just required more land for encampments and inferred that they would not act aggressively unless molested by Confederate troops. Later, on 24 May, Cary returned to Fort Monroe to retrieve the escaped slaves. He demanded the return of Colonel Mallory's property, citing the Fugitive Slave Law as justification.

Realizing that these slaves were being used to build nearby Confederate fortifications on Sewell's Point, Butler refused Cary's request. He informed Cary that since Virginia now considered itself an independent nation, his

Colonel Charles King Mallory, 115th Virginia Militia Regiment, 1860. *Courtesy of the Hampton History Museum.*

"constitutional obligations" under the Fugitive Slave Act were null and void. Butler further noted that because Virginia was at war with the United States he intended to take possession of whatever property his troops required. Since slaves were "chattel property," Butler called Mallory's runaways "contraband of war" and assigned them to support Union operations. It was the Civil War's first step toward becoming a war about freedom.

Even though Butler's "Contraband of War" decision brought slavery to the forefront as a wartime issue, the crafty Union general preferred to focus on his military operations. Ben Butler had been instructed by Winfield Scott to act with "boldness" in his operations against local Confederates. He decided to counter the newly constructed Confederate fortifications on Sewell's Point, Craney Island and Pig Point by occupying Newport News Point. A strong Union base at that point, Butler rationalized, would contest the Confederate positions, threaten Gosport Navy Yard and gain control of the James River channel, cutting riverine communications between Richmond and Norfolk. Accordingly, he sent an expedition under the command of J. Wolcott Phelps, who had just been promoted to brigadier general, to establish an entrenched camp on Newport News Point. Phelps loaded his old regiment, now commanded by Lieutenant Colonel Peter Washburn, along with the 7th New York and 4th Massachusetts, on board the steamers *Monticello* and *Cataline*. The expedition, escorted by the gunboat USS *Pawnee*, landed unopposed on the afternoon of 27 May. The Federals immediately began building an "entrenched camp." Butler considered Newport News Point to be a very strategic site, as he advised Winfield Scott:

The expedition to Newport News…landed without opposition. I have caused an entrenched camp to be made there, which, when completed, will be able to hold itself against any force that may be brought against it, and afford an even better depot from which to advance than Fortress Monroe. The advantages of the News are these: There are two springs of very pure water there; the bluff is a fine, healthy location. It has two good, commodious wharves, to which steamers of any draught may come up at all stages of the tide; it is a new point of operation as Fortress Monroe…a force there is a perpetual threat to Richmond.[9]

Union soldiers constructing earthworks at Camp Butler on Newport News Point, 1861. *Courtesy of Virginia War Museum.*

The entrenched position was named Camp Butler and armed with four eight-inch Columbiads. Private William Osborne of the 4th Massachusetts noted:

> *As soon as Colonel Phelps arrived, he began the construction of the earthworks. These were of semicircular form, terminating at either extremity on the bank of the river, and were nearly a half mile long. In the ditch in front of the works were placed obstructions…On the main works commanding the plain and forest were mounted a number of heavy guns, while on the bluff facing the river was a battery of five large pieces and among them a Sawyer and James rifle. Upon these works the men…labored for many days, and at a time when the weather was extremely hot.*[10]

Butler believed that from his new base at Newport News he could easily capture the Confederate batteries at Pig Point and Suffolk, thereby severing Norfolk's railroad ties to Richmond, causing that port to surrender.

Union reinforcements continued to arrive at Old Point Comfort. On 26 May 1861, one of the most heralded and colorful units landed on the

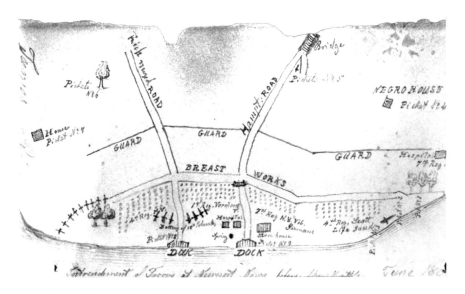

Camp Butler, Newport News Point, map, 1861. *Courtesy of The Casemate Museum.*

Unidentified soldier, 5th New York,
Duryee's Zouaves, 1861. *Courtesy of
the Pohanka Collection.*

Peninsula: the 5th New York Volunteer Infantry, also known as Duryee's Zouaves. The Zouave craze had arrived in America during the late 1850s. The French Imperial Army had integrated North African soldiers into its ranks during the French conquest of Algeria. These Algerian fierce fighters were known as "Zouaoua," and this name was modified in French as "Zouave." Zouaves were known as intrepid warriors and colorful dressers. Soon, numerous French army units were established wearing the distinctive Zouave dress: a short collarless jacket with braid; a sleeveless vest; baggy, voluminous trousers; a twelve-foot-long sash; white canvas leggings; and a tasseled fez or turban wrapped around for dress occasions. During the Crimean War, the Zouaves participated and earned everlasting fame resulting from daring bayonet charges against Russian fixed fortifications defending Sebastopol. Captain George B. McClellan, an official U.S. Army observer of the siege, called Zouaves "the finest light infantry that Europe can produce...the beau-ideal of a soldier."[11]

When war clouds threatened the United States, numerous volunteer and militia regiments were organized in both the North and South. One of the most publicized units was the Duryee's Zouaves. On 12 April 1861, several Unionists gathered in Manhattan to join a volunteer regiment for two years' service. This unit was originally named Advance Guard, and Colonel Abram Duryee was selected as its commander. A wealthy mahogany importer with over three decades of service in the 7th New York Militia, Duryee decided that the unit would be outfitted as Zouaves. Duryee's fame attracted New York's elite to the regiment. Lawyers, businessmen, veterans of foreign campaigns, volunteer firemen and the socially elite flocked to join the unit. Several very experienced officers, including West Point graduates Lieutenant Colonel Gouverneur Kemble Warren and Captain Judson Kilpatrick, were assigned leadership positions within the regiment. Duryee sought to forge a highly disciplined, professional unit and enlisted only those individuals who were physically imposing and educated. He desired that his unit bring great glory to the state of New York. The Zouaves trained at Fort Schuyler until they received orders to Virginia. The 5th New York marched through the city to Broadway, where the streets were thronged with people waving flags and shouting encouragement. Once the regiment reached City Hall Park, all 848 men participated in a Zouave drill as the spectators looked on with admiration. Duryee's command then marched down to the pier and

Left: Colonel Abram Duryee, 5th New York, circa 1860. *Courtesy of the Schroeder Collection.*

Below: Duryee's Zouaves. *Courtesy of The Casemate Museum.*

embarked on the steamer *Alabama* to Old Point Comfort. Steak sandwiches from Delmonico's were issued to the men to enjoy during their crowded trip south. Upon arriving in Virginia, they were met by cheers and acclaim that the "red-legged devils" would put an end to secessionism. Duryee's command then went into camp surrounding Joseph Segar's mansion, overlooking the Chesapeake Female College on Strawberry Banks.

By the end of May, another unique unit arrived that would strengthen Butler's command to over six thousand men: Bartlett's Naval Brigade. This unit was assigned to the Rip Raps (Fort Calhoun) and became disorganized when its commander was injured in a fall. Eventually, the unit was reorganized as the Union Coast Guard.

Several other New York regiments also arrived on the Peninsula by early June. When the war erupted, the state of New York placed the call for volunteers, and the response was overwhelming. Units were formed in major population centers and received nicknames like the Troy Regiment, as the 2nd New York was formed in that city. The 3rd New York Volunteer Infantry Regiment was also known as the Albany Regiment. Colonel Frederick Townsend began to organize this regiment even before President Lincoln called for seventy-five thousand volunteers. Townsend wrote John Germond Butler:

> *The time has at length arrived for patriots to turn out in the service of the country. I have received such assurances from a high official source in Washington, as to lead me to conclude that if I raise a regiment it will be accepted into the service of the United States, and I have now time to say to you that it afford me great pleasure if would undertake to raise a company in Syracuse, and, as its commanding officer, accompany me.*[12]

Butler replied that he already had a company ready to join the 3rd New York known as the Syracuse Zouaves.

John Butler had created his unit following the concepts of Elmer Ellsworth of the Ellsworth Zouaves. Butler's men were held to a strict moral code, and the *Syracuse Journal* noted that "Captain Butler...in every discipline has shown himself the model for his young comrades to copy. Courteous, magnanimous, and kind, he has attracted his associates to him by the strongest bonds of friendship and respect."[13] The unit left Syracuse with great fanfare. Ladies pinned Union rosettes to each soldier's jacket. A ceremony was held where a U.S. flag was presented to the Zouaves, and Butler thanked the assemblage with comments of thanks: "In behalf of the company I thank you…for this distinguished token of their favor. My heart is too full for utterance, but I will testify by my acts how much I love my country. I will defend the flag to the last, and it shall be returned to you unsullied, with not a star dimmed, not a stripe diminished."[14]

The Syracuse Zouaves were smartly clad in an exotic uniform composed of "loose trousers with white leggings, a close-fitting light blue shirt trimmed with a yellow braid, a dark blue jacket, also trimmed with yellow. They also wore a dark blue cap trimmed with gold lace, and added to their outfit a rolled red blanket that was attached to their knapsacks."[15]

When these Zouaves arrived in Albany, they were mustered into the 3rd New York as Company D on 14 May 1861. The entire regiment was then sent to New York City, where they received Enfield rifled muskets with bayonets. On 3 June, the 3rd New York boarded the steamer *James Alger* and arrived at Fort Monroe the next day.

Another regiment quickly organized in New York City was the 7th New York Volunteer Infantry Regiment. The 7th New York, along with the 8th New York, composed New York's "German Corps." These regiments contained mostly German natives who had come to the United States following the failed 1848 revolution in Germany. The Steuben Guards, as the 7th New York was called, mustered into service on 23 April 1861. Unfortunately, they were poorly equipped, as a letter to the *New York Times* on 1 May 1861 noted:

I have seen no troops before, and I have seen none since, in which there was the same indescribable aspect of discipline. The men were not in uniform, but very poorly dressed—in many case with "flip-flop" shoes. The business—like air with which they marched rapidly through the deep mud of Third Avenue was the more remarkable.

With "one of two exceptions" almost every officer then in the regiment had experience in European armies, and six out of eight of the soldiers had seen service, often in battle. The only arms they have as yet are a few old muskets brought by the officers themselves.[16]

The correspondent also noted that tailors within the regiment had to re-sew uniforms and put buttons on them. Colonel Joseph Carr of the 2nd New York also complained about "the dishonesty of the contractors." Carr noted:

Some of the clothing issued to the men during the early days of the Civil War was made of the vilest "shoddy" and literally fell from their bodies. In Fort Monroe men in the 2nd New York Volunteers appeared on parade with blankets wrapped around them to conceal a lack of proper garments, and sometimes stood sentinel with naked feet and naked bodies. [17]

The 7th New York, however, was eventually fully armed, uniformed and equipped with knapsacks, haversacks, canteens, blankets and overcoats. Colonel John Bendix received a silk regimental flag as a gift from the great-granddaughter of a Revolutionary war hero, Baron von Steuben. The unit embarked on the steamer *Empire City* for Fort Monroe singing German songs like "Jubuellerah."

Following the 1st Vermont's march into Hampton, Colonel Ewell ordered Hampton abandoned and the bridge burned. As Ewell continued to struggle with all of his responsibilities, Colonel John Bankhead Magruder arrived at Yorktown aboard the steamer *Logan* to assume command of the Peninsula.

Camp of Weber's Turner Rifles. *Courtesy of Virginia War Museum.*

Magruder immediately realized that he needed time to organize his command, establish a system of defense and gather more troops. Thus, he began his almost daily bombardment of reports and requests entreating that more troops, weapons, supplies and artillery be sent to defend the Peninsula. On 24 May, he demanded reinforcements, writing: "I shall need at least four companies of cavalry to operate against the advance of troops against Hampton, to cut off their parties, to harass them on the march, and to beat up their quarters."[18] Magruder further advised Richmond:

> *When I took command there were no works on the James River below Jamestown, no fortifications at Williamsburg, Yorktown or Gloucester, with the exception of one gun at Yorktown and perhaps two at Gloucester Point. I had to defend a Peninsula 90 miles in length and some 10 miles in width, enclosed between two navigable rivers, terminated by a fortress impregnable as long as the enemy commanded the waters.*
>
> *I…made a tow on horseback of the lower part of the Peninsula, in order to get some knowledge of the country. Seeing at a glance that three broad rivers could not be defended without fortifications, and that these could ever be built if the enemy knew our weakness and want of preparation, I determined to display a portion of my small force in his immediate presence, and forthwith selected Bethel as a place at which a small force could best give him battle should he advance.*[19]

Prince John believed that with twenty-five thousand men arrayed along fortifications built defending the York River at Yorktown and Gloucester Point and "at the mouth of the Warwick River, and at Mulberry Island Point, and the redoubts extending from the Warwick to James River,"[20] he could hold off the advance of any enemy force.

What Magruder needed most of all was time and men. He knew that the ever-growing Union force at Fort Monroe, supported by additional Federal gunboats, would give Butler an advantage to flank his main defensive line before his fortifications could be built. Magruder decided to play for time by baiting Butler into attacking an advance defensive position. Prince John selected Big Bethel Church, a crossroads behind a bend in the northwestern branch of the Back River (also known as Brick Kiln Creek), thirteen miles below Yorktown and eight miles from Hampton, as the place to provoke

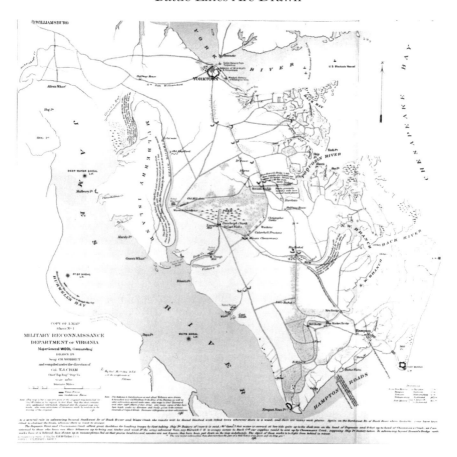

The Peninsula, Thomas Cram, map, 1861. *Courtesy of Lee Hall Mansion.*

an attack. General Robert E. Lee agreed with Magruder's plan to block the advance of the aggressive Federal forces, noting: "I take pleasure in expressing my gratification at the movements that you have made, and hope you might be able to restrict the advance of the enemy and securely maintain your own position."[21]

Before Magruder could establish any forward position, he needed to handle the flow of refugees streaming up the Peninsula. When Butler occupied Newport News Point, John Baytop Cary and his command abandoned Hampton, which caused great concern among the civilian population. They had lived in fear since Federal troops began arriving at Fort Monroe and must decide whether to abandon their homes and move up the Peninsula's

Colonel Abram Duryee and his officers on the front porch of the Segar mansion, 1861. *Courtesy of the Pohanka Collection.*

two primary roads to Yorktown or Williamsburg or take a ship elsewhere. Magruder noted from Yorktown that "the women and children have been passing here all day from Hampton, and Major Cary is also retreating on this place with about sixty-five men, out of two hundred...the remainder of his men being occupied attending to their families."[22]

When the Duryee's Zouaves arrived on the Peninsula, they witnessed the flight of Joseph Segar's family. Segar, a staunch Unionist and former member of the Virginia General Assembly, left behind his elegant manor house, orchards, farm fields and the grand Hygeia Hotel on Old Point Comfort in fear of what the Federal soldiers might do to his family. As soon as he was gone, his home was occupied and stripped of everything. Despite Colonel Duryee's proclamation that all property rights would be respected, Hampton was virtually empty. One Zouave, Thomas Southwick, noted that the "houses I passed were all deserted, not a sound was heard and I felt sick at the heart and deplored the horrors of war. God grant that the owners may be able to return to their homes."[23]

On Newport News Point, the Parker West family was surrounded by Federal troops on 27 May. Even though a guard of Vermont volunteers protected their home, the Wests lived in fear and witnessed the Federal soldiers plundering surrounding farms and homesteads, despite strict orders against pillaging. The Wests secured a pass from General Phelps, loaded up their belongings in several carts and headed toward Williamsburg. As they passed up the Peninsula, they found most of the homes and fields abandoned. Magruder encountered the West family, and George Benjamin West remembered their conversation:

> *After breakfast we…met General Magruder near the picket, with some cavalry, reconnoitering. He stopped and inquired as to the number and position of the Yankees—whether they had thrown up entrenchments— and intimating that he would attack them. He seemed to feel very sorry for father and told him to go to Yorktown, and he would furnish us with quarters and would supply all our wants as long as he had anything to eat himself. We have always felt very…grateful to him for his kindness and offer, and in fact, he was kind to all of the refugees and did all in his power to help them.*[24]

The exodus of civilians up the Peninsula and Butler's aggressive movements had pushed the Federal lines to Newmarket Creek. This display of Federal power prompted local recruitment. Ewell was able to muster

Captain Francis Lightfoot Lee, Lee Guards, circa 1861. *Courtesy of Virginia War Museum.*

numerous units such as the Warwick Beauregards, Hampton Grays, York Rangers, Washington Artillery, Old Dominion Dragoons, Lee Guards, Peninsula Artillery and the Wythe Rifles. The Wythe Rifles had been formed by Captain William Royall Willis in June 1859. Many of the soldiers were students from the Hampton Military Academy and were trained under the guidance of W.E. Cutshaw. The Wythe Rifles were the best-armed and uniformed unit on the Lower Peninsula. They had been issued Model 1855 rifled muskets. Their uniform was a dark blue frock coat trimmed in green and Hardee hats. Many of the units marched to Cape Page in Williamsburg to receive instruction.

While the recruitment of local soldiers was critical to Magruder's defensive plans, he still needed more trained troops. His requests to Richmond finally paid dividends when, on 24 May 1861, the 1st North Carolina Volunteer Infantry Regiment arrived at Yorktown.

The 1st North Carolina was the first unit from North Carolina to arrive in Virginia. The unit was commanded by Colonel Daniel Harvey Hill, former superintendent of the North Carolina Military Institute in Charlotte. Hill, a native of South Carolina, graduated in USMA's class of 1842. He had served with distinction during the Mexican War and brevetted to the rank of major. D.H. Hill resigned his commission in 1849 to teach mathematics at Washington College in Lexington, Virginia, until 1854, when he assumed the same position at Davidson College in North Carolina. Hill, a fervent Presbyterian, married Isabella, the daughter of a well-known church leader, Reverend Robert Morrison. Isabella's sister was Mary Anna, who later married Thomas Jonathan Jackson. While at Davidson, Hill entered a literary phase. He published one textbook, *Elements of Algebra*, and two religious tracts, *A Consideration of the Sermon on the Mount* and *The Crucifixion of Christ*. These works presented Hill's multifaceted intelligence and broad-based knowledge. *Elements of Algebra* presents an excellent understanding of the topic as well as his Southern nationalism. His anti-Northern propaganda could be seen in many of the questions: "The field of battle at Buena Vista is 6½ miles from Saltillo. Two Indiana Volunteers ran away from the field of battle at the same time; one ran half a mile per hour faster than the other, and reached Saltillo 5 minutes and 54 6/11 seconds sooner than the other. Required their respective rates of travel."[25] Other questions detailed Yankee trickery, fraud and so forth,

Daniel Harvey Hill, 1st North Carolina. *Courtesy of The Casemate Museum.*

as well as always placing Southerners in a favorable light. The textbook obviously did not sell well in the North.

In 1858, Hill's dreams of establishing a military academy in North Carolina were fulfilled when he was named superintendent of the new North Carolina Military Institute in Charlotte. Hill also served as professor of mathematics and artillery, as well as president of the board of directors. The school was organized much like the U.S. Military Academy and served 140 students by the spring of 1861.

When war erupted, Hill was named colonel of North Carolina Volunteers and placed in command of Camp Ellis, near Raleigh. Hill supervised the camp's instruction and organized various militia units into regiments. When Adjutant General John F. Hoke organized the 1st North Carolina Regiment, he named Colonel D.H. Hill as the unit's commander. Fellow West Point graduate and North Carolina Military Institute faculty member Charles C. Lee was named the unit's lieutenant colonel, and James H. Lane, also an NCMI faculty member and Virginia Military Institute graduate, was named regimental major. Lee had already served his state when he was on a mission in March to purchase weapons from Northern manufacturers.

The 1st North Carolina included ten companies from throughout the state, including units like the Edgecombe Guards, Charlotte Greys, Fayetteville Independent Light Infantry, Enfield Blues, Hornets Nest Rifles and Southern Stars. The Fayetteville Independent Light Infantry, founded in 1793, was the oldest military unit in the state, whereas the Charlotte Greys was a company composed of students from the North Carolina Military Institute. The Greys were called the "Boy Company," as no member, including the company commander Captain Egbert Ross, was over twenty years old.

Hill's regiment was the only unit ready to answer the call for troops to defend the Confederacy's new capital at Richmond. The 1st North Carolina left Raleigh with great fanfare and received equal applause when they arrived in Petersburg. The first companies went into camp outside of Richmond until the regiment was fully assembled. When the Federals had briefly occupied Hampton, the Confederacy realized that one of the greatest defensive needs was the Peninsula. Accordingly, Harvey Hill's command entrained to West Point, where they boarded the steamer *Logan* to Yorktown. Yorktown was

Major General John Bell Hood, 1862. *Courtesy of The Museum of the Confederacy.*

considered a "post of honor and danger."[26] Therefore, the morning following their evening arrival, the men were put to work rebuilding the fortifications originally constructed by Lord Cornwallis in 1781.

Additional troops began to arrive to strengthen Magruder's command. The 3rd Virginia (later redesignated as the 15th Virginia) arrived from Richmond via the *Glenlove*. The *Glenlove* struck the gunboat *Patrick Henry* as the steamer left the wharf, and one man fell overboard. Despite this incident, the 3rd Virginia, composed of companies raised in Richmond and Henrico County, disembarked at Grove Wharf and King's Mill Wharf. The men marched to Williamsburg. Colonel Thomas B. August, regimental commander, established his headquarters on the campus of the College of William and Mary. August was a prewar lawyer and had served as adjutant of the 1st Virginia Volunteers during the Mexican War. While August stayed in Williamsburg, Lieutenant Colonel William D. Stuart took several companies and joined Magruder in Yorktown. Also arriving in Yorktown was Montague's Battalion from Essex County. Major Edgar B. Montague was a graduate of the College of William and Mary and had three companies of men.

By early June, Magruder had over 3,400 troops under his command. He placed his artillery under the leadership of George Wythe Randolph and three cavalry companies under the guidance of Major John Bell Hood. Hood, an 1853 West Point graduate, was given an in-the-field promotion to the rank of major to ensure that he outranked the other company commanders. Since Butler, too, had received additional reinforcements and had become very aggressive, Magruder deemed it time to establish his forward position at Big Bethel.

Chapter 4

Planning and Approach

B en Butler's ever-increasing troop strength convinced him to consolidate his control of the Lower Peninsula. Numerous patrols and forays went out from Union lines during early June to probe the countryside to Newmarket Creek and beyond. On 4 June 1861, Butler sent Colonel Allen's 1st New York to the fishing hamlet of Fox Hill, near the mouth of the Back River. Fox Hill was located five miles from Fort Monroe. When a report arrived indicating that part of the 1st New York had been captured, several Zouave companies were sent to rescue their fellow New Yorkers. When they arrived at Fox Hill, no 1st New York or Confederates were to be found. Lieutenant George Duryee took several men to secure boats when a courier arrived and advised that the 1st New York had returned safely into Union lines via the Back River Road. The 5th New York then took a different route back to their camp on Segar's Farm via Hampton. As the Zouaves marched through the virtually abandoned town, a spent ball struck a New Yorker, Lieutenant Barnett, in the right breast, inflicting a slight wound. The Zouaves continued back to camp.

The next day, another alarm was sounded that the 1st New York, which had occupied Hampton that morning, was under attack. Duryee's men rushed toward the town until word came that it was a false alarm. The Zouaves had scouted beyond Newmarket Creek as far as the northwest branch of the Back River, Brick Kiln Creek. There they discovered a small unpainted clapboard church known as Big Bethel. The Federals defaced the sides of the church with graffiti stating "Down with the Rebels! Death to the Traitors."[1]

Right: Colonel William H. Allen, 7th New York Volunteer Regiment. *Courtesy of U.S. Military History Institute.*

Below: Union soldiers raiding along the Back River, 1861. *Courtesy of The Casemate Museum.*

Lieutenant Colonel Warren decided to take a different route back to Union lines, which he believed to be a shortcut. When they reached Newmarket Creek, they discovered the bridge, New Bridge, burned. Warren formed a human chain using his tallest men and best swimmers to help transfer weapons and accoutrements, as well as the men who swam across the creek. Just as they were crossing, a heavy thunderstorm erupted and "we were treated to a magnificent shower bath."[2] Private McIlvaine commented that on "getting out [of the creek] our Zouave costumes & haversacks held so much water I could scarcely stand." Despite the discomfort of the rain and creek crossing, "most of the men found themselves refreshed and less fatigued after the swim than before it."[3]

Captain Judson Kilpatrick had been training his company of Zouaves rigorously since the 5th New York's arrival on the Peninsula. As he sought to instruct his men, he wanted his men to like and respect him. He held mule cart races and, despite Butler's orders against foraging, allowed his men to supplement their rations with food taken from nearby farms. Kilpatrick thought it was another way to make war upon the secessionists. Colonel Joseph Carr of the 2nd New York noted that it was "a well-known fact that the Zouaves' rations [were supplemented with] chicken, roast pig, ham, corn, and other first class foods."[4] On 2 June, Kilpatrick had taken forty men and skirmished with Confederates striving to burn Newmarket Creek Bridge. The Zouaves collected some booty, including "one horse, a harness, three mules, four drums, some grain and a few hams."[5] When Kilpatrick marched his "victorious" men back through Hampton, he gave a patriotic speech that appeared on the front page of the *New York Times*.

Local residents continually complained to General Butler about the Union soldiers' constant search for food and unnecessary vandalism. Many soldiers felt that they had no alternative, as their rations were irregularly issued and when they did receive food it was often "unwholesome and repellent." This situation, despite orders to the contrary, tempted many Union soldiers to glean whatever they needed from the local "secesh." On one march through the countryside, Private Karl Ahrendt of the 5th New York came across the home of a prewar acquaintance from Norfolk. The tobacco-chewing mistress gave Ahrendt food with the approbation "what business I had spilling Virginia blood on their soil," Ahrendt recounted, and "begged me to go back to my parents and to drop my wicked plans."[6] Colonel Joseph

Carr remembered one foraging incident when at Camp Butler under the command of General Phelps. Phelps, according to Carr, was "cool and capable, he was thoroughly liked by his men and by his superior officers. He spoke with a long, drawling 'Yankee' accent, and his piquant sayings were very entertaining." Carr recalled that Camp Butler became alive with "commotion and excitement owing to firing in the direction of our pickets, General Phelps, not excited in the least degree, walked into the writer's tent and said, 'Carr, that's not picket shooting. It is your men shooting p-e-e-g-s.' His surmise proved correct."[7]

Butler and Phelps both took action against pillaging. On 6 June 1861, Surgeon Alonzo M.F. Eisenlord of the 7th New York was dismissed from the service. He had been convicted by court-martial of conduct unbecoming an officer and gentleman for taking money (two one-dollar bills) from a bureau in the West family home on Newport News Point. While similar acts of theft and vandalism were punished, much of the foraging was overlooked unless it involved property owned by a Unionist.

Duryee's Zouaves in camp at Segar Farm. *Courtesy of The Casemate Museum.*

Despite Union soldier complaints that the "men here are treated shamefully—sometimes getting nothing to eat for a whole day at a time," it was generally considered poor management of the commissary. Lieutenant William H. Mallory noted in a letter to his parents that the men "have fish of every kind and oysters and clams in abundance, fresh eggs, ham and potatoes, besides the regular rations." The officers enjoyed their days at the Segar mansion. Mallory remembered the idyllic scene:

> *I often sit on the front piazza just at sunset to muse and enjoy a quiet cigar with a brother officer. The band is playing in the adjoining garden, such opera airs as we are wont to hear in the Academy of our city home; the birds are singing their good night song, and after the beat of the "tattoo" at the camp a little distance behind the mansion…and nothing seen in the curling smoke of meerschaums and cigars but dreams of peace and happiness.*[8]

Mallory was a staff officer, and while he was enjoying the tranquil setting, other members of the Union command sought to expand their control to Newmarket Creek and beyond.

Officers at dinner, Duryee's Zouaves at Segar Farm. *Courtesy of The Casemate Museum.*

The Union navy was also probing the Confederate defenses at the western end of Hampton Roads. Major General Walter Gwynn had designed and constructed a water battery at Pig Point guarding the entrance to the Nansemond River. The battery was commanded by Commander Robert Pegram, CSN, and he had pressed the services of the infantrymen from the Portsmouth Rifles as artillerists. On the morning of 5 June, they were tested by the gunboat *Harriet Lane*, a former Revenue Cutter Service steamer with one XI-inch Dahlgren and four thirty-two-pounders. The *Harriet Lane* fired thirty-three rounds at Pig Point and damaged one of the battery's IVI-inch guns. The battery managed twenty-three shots in reply, which eventually drove the *Harriet Lane* off. Pegram praised his men, noting that they "behaved in the most spirited and creditable manner, and were so regardless of danger that I had often to interpose my authority to prevent their exposing themselves unnecessarily to the enemy's fire."[9]

Meanwhile, Magruder's men were also on the move. The 1st North Carolina had spent their first days at Yorktown constructing entrenchment. Yorktown was considered key to the Confederate ability to retain the Peninsula, and all of the Union naval activity threatened this position. The colonial seaport was the York River gateway to Richmond. Magruder decided that as his troop strength increased, he needed to counter the Federal army's movements up the Peninsula. Consequently, Magruder ordered the 1st North Carolina forward toward Hampton on 30 May, and after a march of four miles, they were ordered back. Again, on 3 June, one company was sent marching toward Hampton until recalled. Hill was dismayed by these orders and wrote his wife Isabella, "Colonel Magruder in command is always drunk and giving foolish and absurd orders. I think that in a few days the men will refuse to obey any order issued by him."[10] Even though there appeared no outward strain between the officers, Magruder recognized the Presbyterian Hill's ambition for advancement and command, and he wrote Richmond that "I think I rank him, but am of the impression that it is the subject of some feeling on his part. He has, however, obeyed my orders so far, and I assume will continue to do so."[11]

Magruder knew, nevertheless, that time for action had come. On 6 June, the Confederate commander detached Montague's Battalion, along with two howitzers and two cavalry companies, to Big Bethel to stop Federal forays toward Yorktown. On his arrival at Bethel, he reported to Magruder

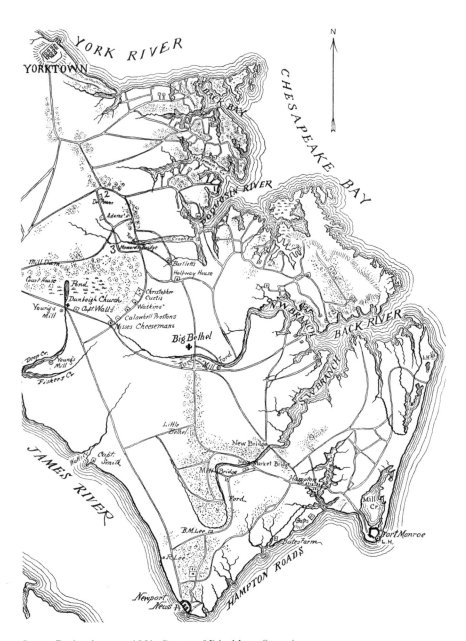

Lower Peninsula, map, 1861. *Courtesy of John Moran Quarstein.*

that his position was about to be turned by Federal forces operating from Newport News Point and up the Poquoson River. Montague ordered a withdrawal to avoid being flanked or captured. As Montague neared Half-Way House on the Hampton-York Highway, he encountered the 1st North Carolina. Magruder had reacted quickly to the rumored Union flanking maneuver and ordered Hill forward to take command at Big Bethel. The North Carolinians were ordered: "Roll blankets, pack three days' rations, and prepare to march."[12] Hill was concerned by these orders, as he knew that it would place his command in a dangerous situation. J.W. Ratchford, aide to D.H. Hill, noted the Confederates' precarious position: "It looked as if Magruder was only sending us down to the vicinity of the fort as a dare to General Benjamin F. Butler. He had no doubt though, that we had sense enough to get out of the way."[13] Magruder wanted to bring on a fight, hopefully to defeat the enemy, but he also wished to give himself time to improve his other defenses.

Hill's task force included 800 men from the 1st North Carolina, the Richmond Howitzers, the Wythe Rifles, four companies from the 3rd Virginia and an additional cavalry detachment. The combined force numbered 1,458 men. Hill ordered Montague to take his battalion to guard the Poquoson River flank. Montague burned Howard's Bridge over the Poquoson River. Meanwhile, Hill marched on to Big Bethel. His men had left Yorktown at 12:30 p.m. and did not arrive at the church until "about dusk." The men had marched almost fifteen miles and had endured a soaking late-afternoon rain. Consequently, they were forced to sleep on the wet ground, without tents. Hampton and the Union army were just over eight miles away. The men, according to Robert Hoke, were forced to "lay on their arms all night."[14]

On 7 June, D.H. Hill made a reconnaissance of the area around Big Bethel. The church was located on the York County side of Brick Kiln Creek where the Hampton-York Highway—commonly known in that part of the Peninsula as the Sawyer Swamp Road or Hampton Road—crossed the stream over a flat wooden bridge. Hill noted that the main approach would come via the Hampton Road, as there was an open field on the Elizabeth City County side of the creek where "masses of the enemy might be readily deployed." Since Hill did not have enough men to cover all of the approaches to Bethel, he decided to build entrenchments. "Presuming that an attempt would be made to carry the bridge across the stream, battery

Fortifications at Big Bethel Church, 1862. *Courtesy of John Moran Quarstein.*

was made for its special protection and Major Randolph placed his guns so as to sweep all the approaches to it," Hill later recounted. The earthwork effectively guarded the road; however, Hill noted that the position would be exposed to fire from "two commanding eminences beyond the creek and on our right."[15] Hill decided that the highest of these, closest to the Hampton Road in Elizabeth City County, must be fortified.

Early in the morning of 7 June, Hill and Lieutenant Colonel Charles Lee laid out the position, and the men began digging earthworks. The work was slow, as there were insufficient axes, picks and shovels. Nevertheless, the men worked in relays while others used branches to build huts. A few complained about the work in the hot June sun; however, most of the men commented about the lack of coffee and meager rations. One Carolinian was able to capture a stray pig, despite Hill's stern admonitions against foraging, and shared it with his mess mates. Another soldier was badly stung striving to retrieve honey from a beehive.

Hill had positioned some cavalry at another church, Little Bethel, just four miles from Hampton. Captain William Werth of the Chatham Grays made a reconnaissance from Little Bethel to Newport News Point on the morning of 7 June to examine the Federal fortifications. Werth was accompanied by Captain Jefferson Curle Phillips and twenty men from the Old Dominion Dragoons and Chatham Grays. As they neared within a few hundred yards of Camp Butler, the Confederates came unexpectedly upon a Union woodcutting detail. One Federal was killed, and the rest rushed back to camp shouting, "Look out for Virginia horsemen!" Two Union companies rushed to the scene, however, and they, in turn, ran back to camp, leaving behind two unlimbered cannon.

On 8 June, an alarm was given that a Union raiding party, elements of Colonel Max Weber's Turner Rifles, had crossed Newmarket Creek. Hill sent Lieutenant Colonel Lee forward with one howitzer and Company F, the Lafayette Light Infantry. Lee sent a shell into the Union ranks that chased the Federals back across the bridge. No sooner had Lee returned to Big Bethel than news arrived that yet another Union force had ventured beyond Newmarket Creek. Major James Lane was sent forward with a howitzer and Company E, the Buncombe Riflemen. Advanced elements of the 2nd New York and the Buncombe Riflemen came within thirty-five yards of each other. When the New Yorkers indicated that they wished to parlay, one soldier stepped forward and stated to Lieutenant George Gregory, "I know that you are friends! I belong to the 2nd New York Regiment." Gregory instantly pulled out his pistol and pointed it at the New Yorker, demanding, "Drop your musket or I'll blow your brains out! You're my prisoner!"[16] The riflemen then poured a volley into the Federals, injuring several New Yorkers. While the 2nd New York returned fire, it had no impact upon the North Carolinians, and the Federals left the field in a rush.

Captain Jefferson Curle Phillips, Old Dominion Dragoons, 1862. *Courtesy of the Hampton History Museum.*

Colonel Max Weber,
Turner Rifles, 1861.
*Courtesy of U.S. Military
History Institute.*

Lane returned to Big Bethel, and his men were jubilant after their "hunting party." They had captured one prisoner, "a stout, ugly fellow" who told his captives that "he had nothing against the South."[17] Hill reported about the Northern casualties after the fight that "reliable citizens reported that two cartloads and one buggy load were taken into Hampton. We had not a single man killed."[18] Hill believed that these skirmishes prompted the Union advance on 10 June.

John Bankhead Magruder arrived at Big Bethel accompanied by his cavalry escort. One officer observed, "Of commanding form and loving display, he had assembled a numerous staff, all, like himself, in the most showy uniforms."[19] Prince John surveyed and approved Hill's dispositions. Magruder seemed pleased with his forward position. He had "showed himself," giving the dare "to any and every Federal commander whose aspirations after early laurels might move him to advance upon the Confederate camp at Big Bethel."[20]

Ben Butler was very ready to pick up the gauntlet thrown down by Magruder. He had reviewed the reports of Confederate aggressive movements between Little Bethel and Newmarket Bridge and decided that he must act. Butler's

Colonel Max Weber's Turner Rifles skirmishing near Newmarket Creek, 1861. *Courtesy of John Moran Quarstein.*

Duryee's Zouaves. *Courtesy of The Casemate Museum.*

aide, Major Theodore Winthrop, a Yale graduate and correspondent for the *Atlantic Monthly*, studied the landscape and approaches to Little Bethel. Winthrop believed that the Confederate position could be easily taken with a surprise dawn attack. He then created a somewhat complex plan of advance:

A regiment or battalion to march from Newport News, and a regiment from Camp Hamilton…Each will be supported by sufficient reserves under arms in camp, and with advanced guards out on the road of march…

At 12, midnight, Colonel Duryee will march his regiment, with fifteen round cartridges, on the country road towards Little Bethel. Scows will be provided to ferry them across Hampton Creek. March to be rapid, but not hurried. A howitzer with canister and shrapnel to go.

A wagon with planks and material to repair the Newmarket Bridge. Duryee to have the two hundred rifles. He will pick the men to whom to entrust them….Newport News movement to be made somewhat later, as the distance is less. As the attack is to be by night, or dusk of morning, and in two detachments, our people should have some token, say a white rag (or dirty white rag) on the left arm…If we bag the Little Bethel men, push on to Big Bethel, and similarly bag them. Burn both the Bethels, or blow up if brick. If we find the enemy and surprise them, men will fire one volley, if desirable, not reload, and go ahead with the bayonet. To protect our rear in case we take the field-position, and the enemy should march his main body (if he has any) to recover them, it would be well to have a squad of competent artillerists, regular or other, to handle the captured guns on the revetment of our main body. Also spikes to spike them if retaken…

Perhaps Duryee's men would be awakened with a new aim in a night or early dawn attack, where there will be little marksman duty to perform. Most of the work will be done with the bayonet, and they are already handy with the old one. [21]

An order of march detailed that Colonel Abram Duryee's 5th New York and Colonel Frederick Townsend's 3rd New York, accompanied by two howitzers, was to be the advance force, with a reserve force, the 1st and 2nd New York, to follow a few hours later from Camp Hamilton. The Camp Butler contingent included Lieutenant Colonel Peter T. Washburn's "New England Battalion," composed of the best men from the 1st Vermont and 4th Massachusetts. Washburn's command was followed by Colonel John E. Bendix's 7th New York with two howitzers, commanded by Lieutenant John Trout Greble of the 2nd U.S. Artillery. The plan dictated that Bendix and Townsend should juncture about a mile and a half from Little Bethel Church and then continue their march toward the Confederate positions.

Colonel William M. Allen, 1st
New York Volunteer Regiment,
1861. *Courtesy of U.S. Military
History Institute.*

One key element of the Union assault plan was the night march.
Federal soldiers wore white armbands to distinguish themselves from
the enemy. Another precaution, the password "Boston," which was to be
announced when unrecognized troops approached, was implemented to
limit confusion.

The entire 4,400-man force was placed under the command of Brigadier
General Ebenezer Weaver Peirce. A *Mayflower* descendant from Freetown,
Massachusetts, Peirce attended Freetown Academy. Prior to the war, he
served in several local offices and as an officer in the Massachusetts State
Militia. He was promoted to brigadier general in 1855. Even though Butler
disliked West Pointers, he had wanted J. Wolcott Phelps, then commander
of Camp Butler, to be in charge of this expedition. Butler knew that Phelps
was the most competent officer available; however, there were several militia

Lieutenant John
Trout Greble,
2nd U.S. Artillery.
*Courtesy of The
Casemate Museum.*

officers on the Peninsula who outranked him. Since Butler "did not deem the enterprise at all difficult,"[22] he believed that Peirce could do the job.

As the Federals organized themselves for their night march, the Confederates continued to improve their Big Bethel position. More spades and shovels arrived that day. Many of the soldiers attended a sermon preached by a Baptist minister from Hampton. Once the worship service was over, the men went back to work improving their earthworks.

Chapter 5

Bloodshed at Bethel

As darkness began to fall that evening, the units assigned to the operation learned their marching orders. Duryee's Zouaves were issued twenty rounds of "buck and ball" cartridges, a day's rations and orders to wrap their white turbans around their left arm. At 9:30 p.m., Judson Kilpatrick took the advance guard of Zouaves from their camp at Segar's Farm to the Hampton River. There his men crossed the river at 10:00 p.m. in scows and began their march toward Little Bethel. The advance guard's primary duty was to capture all citizens or pickets encountered to ensure the element of surprise. Kilpatrick's command was also to secure Newmarket Creek Bridge and then begin a position to attack Little Bethel by 1:00 a.m.

At midnight, Colonel Duryee marched the rest of his command through Hampton en route to Newmarket Creek Bridge. One hour later, Colonel Townsend's 3rd New York followed toward Little Bethel. As these units marched, filling the night's quiet with the tramp of advancing men, Washburn's New England Battalion left Camp Butler. Washburn was followed one hour later by Colonel Bendix's 7th New York.

As Kilpatrick's command neared Little Bethel, Gordon Winslow, the regiment's chaplain, had scouted ahead and discovered a Confederate picket post. Winslow reported this news back to Kilpatrick. The intrepid captain then took eight men forward and surrounded the picket post. Kilpatrick had his men lie on the ground as he walked toward the fire-lit clearing. As the impetuous captain approached, a sentry called out, "Who

Duryee's Zouaves crossing the Hampton River, 1861. *Courtesy of Virginia War Museum.*

goes there? Who stands there?" Kilpatrick replied, "A Virginian!" Kilpatrick then yelled, "Charge!" and his fellow Zouaves fired into the Virginians and rushed them with their bayonets. One Southerner escaped, and the others were captured. While these men were in civilian clothes, they were armed, and the Zouaves referred to one of their captures as "Captain Whiting." Henry Clay Whiting was considered by the Zouaves as a "fine specimen of a Southern soldier, standing six feet in height, it could easily be seen that he was a perfect gentleman, and that he keenly felt his misfortune."[1] Kilpatrick pulled Whiting off his horse and then rode it as he escorted the prisoners to the main body of Zouaves.

As the 5th New York and Washburn's command neared Little Bethel, Colonel Duryee learned of Kilpatrick's episode and feared that it might have alerted the Confederates to the Federal approach. His concerns were needless, as the evening's quiet was filled with the explosion of musketry. Duryee and Washburn believed that the Confederates had assaulted the other Union troops, and their men retraced their path toward the sound of gunfire. When they arrived, they discovered a chaotic scene.

The 3rd New York Regiment was marching into "a defile through a mute wood" when, according to Colonel Frederick Townsend, "a heavy and well-sustained force of canister and small arms was opened up upon the regiment."[2] The New Yorkers were totally surprised, as Townsend knew that he was following Duryee's Zouaves and could not believe that the enemy would be in such a position to fire upon his command. The 3rd New York reeled under the fire, broke ranks and fell into the woods on either side of the road. Townsend reorganized his men and returned fire as they shouted, "Boston!" General Peirce, who was 250 paces ahead of the 3rd New York with his aides, a detachment of the 2nd New York and two howitzers, rushed back to the scene of action. He had passed there only minutes before and had noticed a large number of soldiers. He thought them "to be friends" and passed them by. Peirce and Townsend reorganized the 3rd New York and, under heavy fire, began to withdraw with fixed bayonets. The expedition's commander wanted Townsend's regiment to fall back across Newmarket Creek and burn the bridge with the hopes that the "enemy" would follow and assault the Federal troops in a more favorable defensive position. Washburn and Duryee turned their troops away from Little Bethel and rushed to the sound of musketry. Lieutenant Colonel Washburn suspected that the "skirmish" was friendly fire. When Washburn arrived on the scene, he "immediately formed my command and caused them to shout 'Boston' four times."[3] It was now discovered that the enemy was in fact Bendix's 7th New York. No one had given Bendix the "Boston" password. Furthermore, Bendix understood that the Federals would not use cavalry during this operation; however, the horses used to draw the artillery and carry the officers prompted the 7th New York to unleash their destructive volley into the 3rd New York. It was the first "friendly fire" incident of the Civil War and cost the Union twenty-one casualties.

The combat between the New York regiments had thrown the entire Union column into confusion. Townsend's soldiers, in response to the 7th New York's "ambush," had also fired toward a Zouave platoon escorting Lieutenant Greble's artillery from Newmarket Bridge. Colonel Duryee was actually challenged and almost shot at by members of the 1st Vermont. While none of these incidents caused any mishap, the sight of dead or wounded comrades, shot by their own compatriots, must have been unnerving. As Corporal Edward Wright remembered later, "As I saw the life-blood ebbing from their wounds as they lay stretched out on the stoop of a small farm house nearby, I pitied their sad fate."[4]

Butler's complex plan to capture the two Bethels had backfired and fallen apart. Peirce appeared confused as to what to do next. The militia general held a "council of war." Duryee and Washburn stressed that since the element of

Colonel John E. Bendix, 7th
New York Volunteer Regiment.
*Courtesy of U.S. Military History
Institute.*

surprise had been lost, the advance should be cancelled. Washburn believed that the Confederates would be reinforced from Yorktown; however, Peirce countered that he had already called the 1st and 2nd New York forward from Camp Hamilton to support the Bethel operation. Aides Major Winthrop and Captain Peter Haggerty pushed Peirce to continue the movement. Peirce "decided that it was my duty to follow my written instructions" and advised Washburn, Townsend and Duryee that the Federal troops would follow the original design of General Butler "to the extent of our several abilities."[5]

Peirce ordered that the wounded be returned to Camp Butler and ordered his column forward to Little Bethel. The position had already been abandoned by the Confederates. Peirce ordered the Little Chapel burned and prepared to march forward. He gleaned information from an old woman at a farmhouse and from a "negro" that the Confederate garrison at Big Bethel numbered over four thousand men. Consequently, Peirce sent West Pointers Judson Kilpatrick and Gouverneur Warren on separate, but similar, missions to scout the enemy's Big Bethel position.

When Kilpatrick returned from his scouting mission, he advised Peirce that he "found the enemy with about from three to five thousand men posted in a strong position on the opposite side of the bridge, three earthworks and a masked battery on the right and left; in advance of the stream thirty pieces of artillery and a large force of cavalry."[6] Kilpatrick believed that Big Bethel was an extremely strong position. Gouverneur Warren, a former topographical engineer, disagreed with Kilpatrick's assessment and thought that the Confederate fortifications held fewer than two thousand men. He believed that the Confederate left could easily be turned. Warren furthermore advocated that the forward battery on the south side of Brick Kiln Creek was one of the "commanding eminences" and should be captured. Although the Federals realized that the

Captain Judson Kilpatrick, 5th New York, Duryee Zouaves. *Courtesy of the Schroeder Collection.*

element of surprise had been lost, Peirce was convinced that the prospect for victory was within the Union's grasp.

While the Federals had fought themselves and pondered their movement, the Confederates had been preparing for battle. At 3:00 a.m. on 10 June, Magruder ordered the 1st North Carolina to march on Little Bethel and thence to Newmarket Creek. The drumroll awakened the soldiers. They quickly donned their gear and were ready to march. Magruder and Hill led the six hundred Carolinians and three guns, manned by the Richmond Howitzers, down the Hampton Road until they met a lady, Mrs. Hannah Nicholson Tunnel. Mrs. Tunnel's home near Newmarket Creek Bridge had been occupied by Captain Kilpatrick and his company of Zouaves. They held Hannah's brother-in-law, Mr. Robert Tunnel, prisoner. Once the Federals became embroiled in their friendly firefight, Hannah Tunnel had slipped away and rushed through the woods to avoid detection by the Federals until she reached the road far in advance of the Federal troops. Hannah then came upon the Confederate column about three miles south of Big Bethel. She warned Magruder and Hill that the Federals had over four thousand men marching toward them. Magruder then wheeled his men about and returned to Big Bethel. One member of the Richmond Howitzers, William S. White, later wrote that "all honor is due to a noble hearted Virginia country woman, who undoubtedly saved our camp from surprise and kept the forces sent out early this morning from running into the enemy unawares."[7]

Magruder's prudent decision to fall back on Big Bethel to make a stand behind earthworks against the larger Federal force would give the Confederates a key advantage during the forthcoming battle. Hill deployed the troops, expecting the Federals to arrive on the field at any moment. Lieutenant Colonel William Stuart's companies from the 3rd Virginia, and one howitzer commanded by John Thompson Brown of the Richmond Howitzers, filled the advanced redoubt. Within the woods on the eastern side of the Hampton Road, the Edgecombe Guards (Company A, 1st North Carolina) were positioned. The main redoubt contained four howitzers, three of which commanded the road's approach to the bridge; the other guard, the Confederate right flank. Magruder and Hill then positioned Montague's Battalion, Wythe Rifles and Companies G, H, I, D, C and B, 1st North Carolina, along the interior walls of the main earthwork. In an effort to guard the Confederate left flank, skirmishes from the Wythe Rifles, as well as Companies K and F, were deployed in the woods over one hundred yards beyond the entrenchment. Hood's cavalry was positioned along the road to Yorktown behind the earthwork.

As the hot sun rose into the cloudless sky, D.H. Hill walked among the untried, nervous soldiers, calming them for the engagement that was surely to come, stating, "When you hear the bugle you may know that the enemy is in sight."[8] While the men waited, they took time to improve the earthworks or their forward positions with sassafras boughs. Just before 9:00 a.m., an advanced picket, Private Henry Lawson Wyatt, scampered back into the Edgecombe Guard's skirmish line with news that the enemy was nearby.

Peirce had left Little Bethel with Kilpatrick's company of Duryee's Zouaves in the advance. Once the Federals reached just over one thousand yards from Big Bethel, Peirce formed his troops into a line of battle. Duryee's Zouaves were on the south side of the Hampton Road, and Washburn's New England Battalion was placed to the east of the New Yorkers. On the

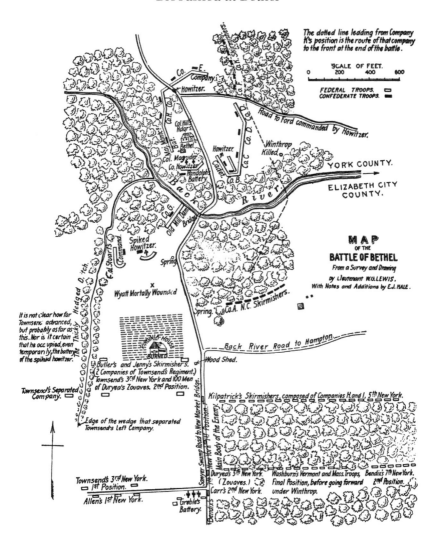

Big Bethel Battlefield, 1861. *Courtesy of John Moran Quarstein.*

left of the road, Townsend's 3rd New York and Bendix's 7th New York were in position. The Federals then began their deliberate march toward the Confederate fortifications. Just after 9:00 a.m., the Federals came in sight of the Confederates. It was an impressive array, with bayonets glittering in

View of Bethel Battlefield, 1861. *Courtesy of The Casemate Museum.*

the sun and the star-spangled banner waving over the heads of the Union soldiers. The scene was immediately disrupted when Major George Wythe Randolph fired a Parrott shell right into the front of Bendix's command. Bendix lamented that even before his command "had got ready for action the enemy opened their fire upon us, striking one man down by my side at the first shot."[9]

Randolph's well-aimed shell opened the first engagement of the war and prompted the men of the 7th New York to fall into the woods to act as skirmishers. Eventually, Bendix's regiment moved onto the Union left and operated adjacent to Washburn's command.

Meanwhile, Peirce pushed Greble's three-gun battery forward, and during the next hour, an artillery duel ensued. Greble's shells whizzed through the main Confederate redoubt and beyond. The elevation was generally too high; however, Major Montague had a shell pass between his horse's front and hind feet and others fly near his head. The rain of shot, shell and canister had little effect upon the entrenched Confederates, and somehow no one was injured. Captain Benjamin Husk remembered one of his soldiers confess, "Colonel

Hill knows [more] about good [breastworks] and ditches than I do, and I'll never grumble again about throwing dirt."[10] Hill eased his soldiers during the hour-long artillery exchange with his confident and brave demeanor. The Mexican War veteran stood in the open calmly smoking a short pipe and called to his men, "Boys, you have learned to dodge already." Hill added, "I am an old hand at it." He then leaned away from a shell that whizzed past and shook his finger at the Federals, yelling, "You dogs! You missed me that time."[11]

As the Confederate shells whizzed across the battlefield, Lieutenant Colonel Warren organized a skirmish line and pressed the Zouaves forward on both sides of the Hampton Road. Lieutenant Jacob Duryee felt that the "disheartening shrieking sound" of shot flying overhead was "very terrifying."[12] Karl Ahrendt noted that "I thought of my mother, my brothers and sisters and friends. A thousand different thoughts ran through my head. But soon enough I thought about nothing at all anymore except to level my rifle and fire."[13] Warren halted the skirmishers and conferred with Duryee. The skirmishers then fell back upon the regiment in preparation for a concerted advance.

Duryee then pointed his sword at the Confederate earthworks and shouted to his men, "I want every man to do his duty. The eyes of the whole country are upon you. Fire low and be careful of your ammunition."[14] The advance was thrown into disorder by the effective Confederate cannon fire. George Burtis later wrote his brother, "One thing, well worth knowing: I learned to dodge cannon balls…listening attentively for the report, then dropping flat, and lying

Major General Daniel Harvey Hill. *Courtesy of Virginia War Museum.*

Colonel Abram Duryee, 5th New York Volunteer Regiment, circa 1862. *Courtesy of the Pohanka Collection.*

until something whizzed over my head. Each time I expected to be nailed."[15] Not all of the Zouaves practiced this technique, and the unit began to take casualties. Private George Tiebout was the first of the regiment to be killed. Tiebout was struck by a canister ball that tore his heart out. William McIlvane noted that Tiebout "fell at my side without uttering a word, or knowing he was struck."[16] Private James Griggs was cut in two by a cannonball, and a shell fragment knocked the musket out of the hands of Sergeant George Mitchell. Private James Taylor, nephew of the wealthy financier Moses Taylor and known to be "in intelligence and mental ability…far above the ordinary run of young men,"[17] was firing his musket from a prone position when he was accidentally shot through the body, mortally wounded by a fellow Zouave.

The Federals were suffering several losses from the Confederate cannon fire. Judson Kilpatrick noted, "The enemy's fire at this time began to fall on us with great effect. My men were falling one after another."[18] Duryee's Zouaves found cover in some woods on the left side of the Hampton Road. Despite the shelling, Colonel Duryee and several of his officers went from the cover of the woods to plan another assault against the enemy's position. The Confederates, spotting the exposed Federals, sent a round of grapeshot at them. Kilpatrick was hit in the right hip and exclaimed, "Are we going to stay here and be shot down, and do nothing?"[19] The same round of canister wounded Private Thomas Cartwright and tore off Colonel Duryee's right shoulder strap.

Colonel Duryee and his staff went back into the woods; however, his son, Lieutenant Jacob Duryee, decided that the Zouaves should attack. The younger Duryee shouted, "Who will follow me? I will charge the batteries."[20] Kilpatrick and about 250 Zouaves attempted a charge. While Kilpatrick's wound made him weak from loss of blood, he could only go forward with the help of his men. The Zouaves then moved out of the woods, through the peach orchard and into the field in front of the forward battery. The Confederate artillery and musketry was too hot for the Zouaves to go any farther, and they fell back into the woods.

Other Federal units offered their own piecemeal attacks during this phase of the engagement. Townsend sent skirmishers from the 3rd New York forward against the one-gun battery; however, they were unable to make headway against the fierce Confederate resistance. Likewise, Lieutenant Colonel Peter Washburn endeavored to maneuver against the main Confederate redoubt. "The attack by my men was very spirited," he later recounted. "The enemy's fire seemed to be concentrated on us…The enemy brought their artillery to bear on us…I ceased firing and withdrew my men…under the woods."[21]

Charge of Duryee's Zouaves, 10 June 1861. *Courtesy of The Casemate Museum.*

Magruder was directing the adjustment of his command to counter these uncoordinated Federal assaults. Werth's company of Montague's Battalion was reassigned to the Confederate left, and their effective fire blocked the Federals from crossing the creek. The Federals failed to take advantage of their numerical superiority with these limited assaults. D.H. Hill noted that the Federal "organization was completely broken up."[22] There was no concert of action between Peirce's units, North Carolinian B.M. Hord remembered: "A regiment would come up, fire a volley or two, mostly over our heads and precipitately fall back…it seemed that their principle object was simply to get a sight or a shot at a Rebel, then fall back as quickly as possible."[23] As this phase of the engagement concluded, Hill noted that "we were now as secure as at the beginning and as yet had no man killed."[24]

Peirce, perhaps remembering that Gouverneur Warren had earlier advised that the key to the Confederate position was the control of the forward one-gun battery, decided to make a thrust to capture the battlefield's "commanding eminence" and organized another assault with the 5th and 3rd New York. A detachment of Zouaves, personally commanded by Colonel Abram Duryee himself, surged forward toward the battery as Townsend's regiment moved to flank the Confederate right. Several other Zouaves saw the Albany Regiment advance off to their left and approached Lieutenant Jacob Duryee. They demanded, "For God's sake, lead us on!" Duryee responded, "Will you follow?" When the men all shouted, "Yes!" Duryee shouted with a wave of his sword, "I will charge the batteries!"[25] This group of about fifty Zouaves rushed through a peach orchard toward the Confederate battery. Just as all the Zouaves neared the one-gun battery, a priming wire broke in

Last charge of Duryee's Zouaves, 1861. *Courtesy of The Casemate Museum.*

the vent, thereby spiking the gun. Captain J. Thompson Brown withdrew this useless gun. Lieutenant Colonel Stuart reported to Magruder that the Federals were advancing in his front with a heavy force (Stuart estimated to be over fifteen hundred men), and another line of skirmishers was moving onto his right flank. Magruder immediately ordered Stuart to withdraw into the main redoubt next to Montague's position.

A critical moment had arrived for the Confederates. The Zouaves occupied the empty one-gun battery and "everything promised a speedy victory" for the Federals. D.H. Hill quickly reacted to overcome this major threat to the entire Confederate right. He organized a counter attack with Captain John L. Bridgers's Edgecombe Guards, supported by Company C. Bridgers formed his men and then led them in a determined assault. "They advanced calmly," the *Hillsborough Recorder* later reported, "coolly, when at the distance…the Zouaves fired on them…not a muscle was moved, but they leaped right on at the double-quick."[26] Duryee, recognizing that his men had no support by which to counter the bold Confederate charge, ordered his men to fall back. As the Zouaves vacated the battery, the North Carolinians swept into this key position "in a most gallant manner," Magruder later reported. The Confederate commander lauded that Bridgers's Edgecombe Guards retook the battery and "held it until Captain Brown had replaced and put into position another piece…Colonel Hills' judicious and determined action was worthy of his ancient glory."[27] Hill merely reported afterward, "It is impossible to overestimate this service. It decided the action in our favor."[28]

As the Zouaves attacked, captured and retreated from the battery, Colonel Townsend's 3rd New York moved to envelope the Confederate right. Townsend urged his men forward; however, he had already missed his opportunity to consolidate the Union's capture of the one-gun battery. "By the time the regiment had arrived at its position, it had become evident that the right portion of the battery had been strongly reinforced by men from the enemy's left," Townsend later recounted, "and that an effort to take the battery then was useless."[29] Nevertheless, the 3rd New York was still in a position to turn the Confederate left. Unfortunately, a portion of his command had become separated from the main body. Townsend then became alarmed when he saw through the undergrowth and hedges "the glistening of bayonets in the adjoining field," and he believed that his command was being flanked by the enemy and "conceived it to be my duty immediately to retire and repel that advance."[30] Only later, when it was

Battle of Big Bethel, 1861. *Courtesy of John Moran Quarstein.*

too late to press an advance against the Confederate left, did he realize that the enemy was made up of members of his own command.

Meanwhile, Company A, 1st North Carolina, was reinforced in the one-gun battery by Company B, the Burke Rifles, 1st North Carolina, elements of Stuart's 3rd Virginia and a detachment of the Wythe Rifles. D.H. Hill crossed the creek and inspected these units' deployment within the forward Confederate entrenchment. He immediately noticed that several Zouaves had taken cover in an old blacksmith shop and an abandoned house to fire upon the Confederate position. These Zouaves were acting as sharpshooters using the new rifled muskets they had been issued the day before. As Hill walked along the fortification, he passed Captain Bridgers and suggested, "Can't you have that house burned?" Bridgers called for volunteers, and five men stepped forward: Corporal George Williams and Privates Henry Lawson Wyatt, Thomas Fallon, John H. Thorp and R.K. Bradley. Armed with only hatchets and matches, they leaped over the earthwork and dashed toward the building when, according to Private Thorpe, "A volley was fired at us by a company, not from the house, but from the road to the left. As we were well drilled in skirmishing, all of us immediately dropped to the ground, Wyatt mortally wounded. He never uttered a word or groan, but lay limp on his back, his arm extended one knee up and a lot of blood on his forehead as large as a man's fist."[31] The other Carolinians carefully made their way back to the battery. Wyatt's body remained where it was as a grim vision of what could happen when exposed to enemy fire.

The shot that actually struck Wyatt in the forehead is attributed by Sergeant Felix Agnus of the 5th New York to Captain Judson Kilpatrick. Kilpatrick had collapsed from loss of blood during the Zouaves' final movement against the Confederate one-gun battery. Several Zouaves, including Agnus and Corporal Allen Seymour, helped Kilpatrick into a frame house located in front of the Confederate works. Once they had gained cover, Agnus yelled to Kilpatrick, "Captain, the Rebs are coming!" He added,

Private Henry Lawson Wyatt, 1st North Carolina, 1861. *Courtesy of the Hampton History Museum.*

"Can you shoot?"[32] Agnus quickly loaded his and another musket and handed them to Kilpatrick. While the Confederates believed that Wyatt was shot by Zouaves from the other side of the Hampton Road, Agnus claimed that it was Kilpatrick's first shot that mortally wounded the young Confederate soldier. As Wyatt's comrades fell to the ground, the Zouaves abandoned the building. It was a timely escape for Kilpatrick and his companions, as the Richmond Howitzers soon sent a shell into the building that set it ablaze.

Meanwhile, Magruder decided that he needed to protect his right flank along the north side of the creek beyond the one-gun battery. He rode up upon Company 1, Enfield Blues, 1st North Carolina, and asked, "Who commands this company?" "Second Lieutenant Parker," came the reply. Magruder then ordered, "Lieutenant, deploy your men along this swamp as sharpshooters. Protect them as well as you can and keep a sharp lookout to the front, as I expect an attack right in your front." Parker protested that his men could not become sharpshooters, stating, "We are armed with smoothbores, sir." This circumstance was of no concern to Magruder, and he reiterated, "Deploy your men, deploy your men."[33]

While the Confederates adjusted their position, anticipating another attack, Peirce endeavored to strengthen his left and center. Union reinforcements, the 1st and 2nd New York, now arrived on the field. Since Duryee had already reported that his men were spent, General Peirce ordered the 3rd and 5th New York to retire from the front line and replace these units with the 1st and 2nd New York. As he did so, an independent Union assault was being organized against the Confederate left by Lieutenant Colonel Peter Washburn and Major Theodore Winthrop. Washburn and Winthrop brought portions of the 1st Vermont and 4th Massachusetts together to assault the main Confederate position on the north side of Brick Kiln Creek. The New Englanders, followed by Colonel John Bendix's Steuben Regiment, made their way through the tangled woods and found a ford across the dark yet narrow stream. Holding their cartridge boxes and muskets over their heads, they crossed the waist-deep creek.

As the column cleared the swamp and moved toward the main redoubt, they brushed aside the Confederate pickets. The Confederates had white bands around their caps, as did the New Englanders. So as Winthrop's command came upon the Confederates, they shouted, "Don't fire!" as if they were friends. The New Englanders then began "to cheer most lustily" and rushed the earthwork. The Union soldiers believed that the Confederate earthwork was open at its gorge and with a sudden rush they could get inside the entrenchment. The companies B and C, 1st North Carolina, poured deliberately and well directed into the Federals. Magruder, upon hearing a mistaken report that the Union soldiers had carried the Confederate position, then reinforced his troops with portions of companies G, C and H, 1st North Carolina. Major Randolph advised Magruder, "Colonel, the North Carolina boys are doing the prettiest kind of work." Magruder replied, "Then sir they are whipped." Benjamin Huske, who had overheard the conversation, reflected, "The firing was incessant, and the roar awful, but I felt perfectly secure because Colonel Hill was there."[34]

The North Carolinians repulsed the Union attack. Winthrop, however, was not willing to give up. He urged his men forward again toward the main redoubt. In an effort to rally his men for this final charge that he believed

Major Theodore
Winthrop, 1861.
*Courtesy of The Casemate
Museum.*

would carry the day for the Union, Winthrop stood up on a log waving his
sword, shouting, "Come on boys; one charge and the day is ours."[35] He was
immediately shot through the heart and fell dead onto the ground. Many a
Carolinian later claimed that the shot that killed Winthrop was their own;
however, Captain Richard Ashe of Company D, Orange Light Infantry,
1st North Carolina, claimed that the shot was actually fired by his African
American servant, Sam Ashe. Winthrop's death completely demoralized his
troops, and they fell back across Brick Kiln Creek. "This retreat," wrote
D.H. Hill, "decided the action on our favor."[36]

Winthrop's body was left where he fell. As the New Englanders retreated,
they were followed by the 7th New York. Colonel Bendix later reported,
"After firing some time withdraw back into the woods. When we got into the
woods, I found the troops retreating, and followed."[37]

Meanwhile, Peirce realized that the day was lost. His men were utterly
exhausted and thoroughly discouraged. The Massachusetts militia general
ordered the two fresh New York regiments to the front to act as a rear guard

Duryee's Zouaves. *Courtesy of The Casemate Museum.*

as he prepared his command to retreat. Everything would then quickly fall apart for the Federals.

George Wythe Randolph noticed that after the last Union assault, "apparently a re-enforcement, or reserve, made its appearance on the Hampton Road and pressed forward towards the bridge, carrying the United States flag near the head of the column." Randolph rushed to bring up another howitzer to sweep the approach to the bridge with canister; however, before he could do so, other members of his unit used a Parrott gun to drive the Federals back. In the meantime, a howitzer had been brought into the main redoubt by Lieutenant Moseley from the Half-Way House. Randolph, who had learned that sharpshooters were still peppering the Confederate position from the house that Wyatt and his compatriots had tried to burn earlier during the battle, determined to shell the building. The Richmond Howitzers' commander also noted that the Union battery covering the Union retreat was in line with the house. Consequently, he decided to simultaneously shell the Federal artillery position. Randolph remembered,

"After an exchange of five or six shots a shell entered a window of the house, increased the fire already kindled, until it soon broke out into a light blaze, and, as I have reason to believe, disabled one of the enemy's pieces. This was the last shot fired. They soon after retreated and we saw no more of them."[38]

Randolph's last shot killed Lieutenant John Trout Greble. Greble had commanded the Union artillery throughout the entire action, and at the engagement's conclusion he was striving to cover the Federal withdrawal. The last Confederate shell exploded near his gun. A large shell fragment tore off part of Greble's skull and killed him instantly. John Greble died while "nobly fighting his guns" and was lionized for his valor and sacrifice. Lieutenant Greble was the first regular army officer and West Point graduate killed during the

Death of Lieutenant Greble. *Courtesy of The Casemate Museum.*

war. He had commanded with distinction during the battle and was described as possessing "to a notable degree the two qualities most needed at the time, namely, military skill and presence of mind in the face of the enemy."[39]

In the meantime, the Federal retreat had evolved into a confusing rush to reach the Newmarket Creek Bridge. Lieutenant Colonel G.K. Warren of the 5th New York strived to bring some order to the chaos. Warren pleaded with Peirce "to remain and see that the rear was properly attended to";[40] however, Peirce, who it is said had lost "all presence of mind,"[41] thought it was unnecessary for him to do so as he had assigned that duty to the 1st New York. Gouverneur Warren was utterly disgusted by the conduct of Peirce. He already knew that the 1st New York had fallen away from the battlefield with some haste. Accordingly, he organized some men to help him gather up the killed and wounded Union militiamen along the Hampton Road. Warren personally carried Greble's body onto an artillery timber so the dead officer's remains could be removed from the battlefield. One Vermont soldier, Private Reuben Parker, became separated from his unit when he tried to rescue Major Winthrop's body. Parker was captured and exchanged a few days later. Parker claimed that his POW exchange was the first of the Civil War.

Just as the Federals left the battlefield, Coppen's Louisiana Zouaves Battalion arrived to reinforce the Confederate position. Lieutenant Colonel George Auguste Gaston Coppen had received his commission and appointment to raise a regiment of Zouaves directly from President Jefferson Davis. The unit was recruited in New Orleans and contained a variety of nationalities; however, the officers and men were primarily French-born or Creole. Several officers only spoke French. Coppen's Zouaves were first assigned to Pensacola. The urgent need for troops to defend Richmond witnessed these Zouaves being sent to Virginia, with great acclaim, by train on 1 June 1861. They arrived in Richmond on 7 June. The Confederate capital was "thrown into a paroxysm of excitement by the arrival of the New Orleans Zouaves…as unique and picturesque looking Frenchmen as ever delighted the oculars of Napoleon the three." The *Richmond Dispatch* also noted that it appeared that "their principal fare, since leaving Pensacola, has been crackers, cheese and whiskey."[42] The unit was immediately sent to the Peninsula by steamer and arrived in Williamsburg the morning of 10 June. They marched directly to Big Bethel.

William White of the Richmond Howitzers commented that "a Louisiana regiment arrived about one hour after the fight was over. They are a fine-looking set of fellows."[43] Not all agreed. George Wills of the 1st North Carolina noted that the Zouaves "are the worst looking men you ever saw in your live [*sic*] they all had on leggings wore red pants, with about three times as much cloth in them as necessary, and a long red bag for a cap, they burnt black as mulattoes."[44] Unfortunately, they had arrived too late to participate in the battle. Magruder ordered them back to Yorktown, as they were not needed and he still feared that the Federals might make some attempt to make a naval assault up the York or Poquoson River. Meanwhile, Hill had ordered Captain Robert Hoke and his company, the Southern Stars, to investigate whether any Federal sharpshooters had remained behind to guard the Union retreat. Learning that all of the Federals were in retreat, he sent Captain Robert Dorthatt's company of dragoons to harass the Federal retreat as far as Newmarket Creek Bridge. The Hampton Road was littered with equipment. "The enemy in his haste," recounted D.H. Hill, "throw away hundreds of canteens, haversacks, overcoats, etc., even the dead were thrown out of the wagons…the pursuit soon became a chase."[45]

The Federal retreat from Big Bethel was indeed disorganized. Zouave Philip Wilson called it "the most damned disgraceful retreat I ever witnessed, and one for which there was no excuse whatever."[46] "The men were tired, hungry, sick and disheartened," Private Thomas Southwick remembered, "blackened with powder and covered with dirt, but there were no laurel wreaths about their brows."[47] Many Union soldiers had seen enough of the battle, like George Burtis, who later admitted, "I was not at all sorry to hear the order given to retreat."[48]

Most of the Union soldiers were dejected due to the poor leadership or by the sights that they had witnessed. Private Thomas Murphy became horrified when he saw a shell cut down two men. Private David

Private Philip Wilson, 5th New York, 1861. *Courtesy of the Schroeder Collection.*

Thomas Cartwright, 5th New York, Duryee's Zouaves, 1862. *Courtesy of the New York Division of Military and Naval Affairs Collection.*

Treforth's head was "blown about twenty feet from his body." The Zouave was further shocked during the retreat when he passed Greble's body strewn across his cannon with his brains "splattered across the barrel."[49] Murphy was discharged within a month of the battle.

Several Union soldiers were motivated by Lieutenant Colonel Warren's example and stayed behind to help their wounded comrades, despite the horrific scenes they encountered. Private Davenport passed a severed hand found in the dirt, realizing that it belonged to Private John Dunn, who had undergone the first battlefield amputation of the war. The surgery was performed by 5th New York surgeon Rufus H. Gilbert. According to Davenport, Dunn "bore the ordeal stoically."[50] Mortally wounded James Taylor begged his friend William Gilder to leave him by the roadside to make room in the wagon for "someone…who can live and fight again."[51] Gilder sadly complied. Privates Phil Wilson and George Guthrie searched the woods to recover their wounded friend, Thomas Cartwright. Cartwright was found, and Lieutenant Colonel Warren, who was with them, took Guthrie's musket and guarded over the men as they moved Cartwright into a cart. All of the wounded that could be recovered made their way in the rear of the retreat, protected by men from the 2nd, 5th and 7th New York. As he sat in the cart, the wounded Cartwright fired his musket at the Confederate cavalry harassing the withdraw.

Once Warren had done his duty recovering wounded, he rode ahead and organized a naval contingent with boat howitzers to guard Newmarket Creek Bridge. Phelps, who had disapproved of Butler's plan to attack the Bethels

Right: Surgical scene, Duryee's Zouaves, 1861. *Courtesy of the Pohanka Collection.*

Below: Lieutenant Greble's body being removed from the battlefield. *Courtesy of The Casemate Museum.*

and recognized it would only end in failure, sent wagons filled with crackers and pickled herring to feed the worn-out troops as they reached Newmarket Creek. He went among his fellow Vermonters, many of whom were greatly affected by the defeat, advising them that he would personally led them to victory in the next battle. These actions put an end to the "series of errors from the time we left Hampton until our return," Warren later lamented.[52]

Chapter 6

Jubilation and Despair

B ig Bethel was the baptism of fire for a nation newly involved in civil war. The soldiers who had served at Bethel would never forget the rude awakening of shells bursting among the smartly clad Zouaves or how Wyatt's body laid lifeless upon the field. Benjamin Huske remembered that the "scene was one of perfect route, horrible beyond description, men with limbs shot off, brains oozing out and every imaginable horror."[1] Those who were there quickly realized that the war would not be filled with parades and that it would not be over before Christmas. All knew that it would be a bloody, desperate affair.

Nevertheless, Magruder was indeed pleased with his victory at Big Bethel. His command had soundly defeated an army over three times its size. Magruder quickly sent his nephew, George Magruder Jr., to Richmond with two reports announcing his great victory. Even though Prince John realized that the Federals had been utterly repulsed, he also recognized that he was unable to take advantage of the situation and dramatically sweep the Union invaders into the sea. He knew that the Confederate position on the Peninsula was still ever so precarious and that Butler's well-fortified command was continuing to receive daily reinforcements.

Just the day before the battle, 9 June, two additional regiments, 9th New York (Hawkins's Zouaves) and the 10th New York (National Zouaves), had arrived at Fort Monroe. Consequently, within hours of the battle's conclusion, Magruder ordered most of his men, except for a cavalry picket, back to Yorktown. This order upset many a Carolinian soldier after such a victory.

Before Magruder gave these orders, the victorious Confederates wandered about the battlefield and shared stories about their roles in the engagement. Many were saddened by the sight of their fellow compatriot Henry Lawson Wyatt's body lying upon the field. Others walked among the Federal positions. John Thorp commented:

> Around the yard were the dead bodies of the men who had been killed by our cannon, mangled in the most frightful manner by the shells…The gay looking uniforms of the New York Zouaves contrasted greatly with the pale, fixed faces of their dead owners. Going to the swamp through which they attempted to pass to assault our lines, presented another bloody scene. Bodies dotted the black morass from one end to the other. I saw one boyish, delicate looking fellow lying in the mud, with a bullet-hole though his breast. His hand was pressed on the wound from which his life blood had poured; and the other was clenched in the grass that grew near him. Lying on the ground was a testament which had fallen from his pocket, dabbled with blood. On opening the cover I found the printed description, "Presented to the Defenders of their Country by the New York Bible Society." A United States flag also stamped on the page.[2]

When Mary Boykin Chesnut heard this story she wrote in her diary, "How dare they mix the Bible with their own bad passions."

Benjamin Huske also was struck by bodies of the slain Federals. Huske came upon the body of Major Theodore Winthrop. He became especially moved when he examined Winthrop's watch with the pictures of two lovely women inside and thought:

> The death of that poor officer affected me more than anything else, for I knew that there was one home whose light had gone out. Great God! Avert the horrors of this civil war! That we should conquer was all for me while it lasted, a man's blood gets up and he doesn't mind danger. But when the time of action is passed, we feel the truth of what Wellington said, "But one thing is more terrible than victory, and that is defeat."[3]

While these soldiers were truly touched by the pathos of war, others went through the Union jettison found across the battlefield. Many retained souvenirs or found replacement equipment, while others rifled through letters and diaries, laughing as they read words from New York or Massachusetts inquiring if the "Southern barbarians" had been wiped out yet.[4] Some soldiers quickly wrote home to their loved ones reflecting upon the great victory and how they had missed death by inches. Private Lewis Warlick of the 1st North Carolina commented, "I had the but [*sic*] of my gun shot off in my hands." Captain Egbert Ross wrote, "I saw six Zouaves take deliberate aim at me and fire but fortunately they missed me."[5] "Gracious! How the balls showered around us…you can form no idea how they hissed and struck just like a shower of hot stones falling into the water,"[6] Benjamin Huske excitedly recounted. Despite these close calls, most of the Confederates were in "high glee" after the battle. Hill reported that the Confederate soldiers "seemed to enjoy it as much as boys rabbit-shooting."[7] B.M. Hord later remembered that the battle "reminded me more of a lot of boys fighting a bumblebee nest than a real battle."[8]

Confederate map of Big Bethel Battlefield. *Courtesy of The Casemate Museum.*

Southerners rejoiced over the victory as they learned about Big Bethel, and laurels were spread everywhere. The one Confederate killed, Private Henry Lawson Wyatt, achieved martyrdom. He was the first Confederate infantryman killed in battle, and as Magruder later wrote, "Too much praise cannot be bestowed upon the heroic soldier who we lost."[9] Wyatt and his companions had, according to D.H. Hill, "behaved with great gallantry."[10] Wyatt was taken to Yorktown and then to Richmond, where he was buried with great honor.

Hill also reflected on the bravery of all the members of his regiment:

> *There were not quite eight hundred of my regiment engaged in the fight, and not one-half of them drew trigger during the day. All remained manfully at the posts assigned them, and not a man in the regiment behaved badly. The companies not engaged were as much exposed and rendered equal service with those participating in the fight. They deserve equally the thanks of the country.*

D.H. Hill noted that the 1st North Carolina "never had more than three hundred actively engaged at any one time." Nevertheless, he concluded by stating that his men's "patience under trial, perseverance under trial and courage under fire have seldom been surpassed by veteran troops."[11] Magruder added to these accolades, stating, "North Carolinians! You have covered yourself with glory, not only as undaunted in the presence of an overwhelming force bearing yourself with bravery restless but above all with a perfection of discipline in an exciting conflict that was unequaled."[12]

Magruder lauded all of the officers and men who had served at Big Bethel that day. He noted how units like the Wythe Rifles had behaved with gallantry and acknowledged the outstanding service of the Richmond Howitzers. Major George Wythe Randolph, Magruder proclaimed, "has no superior as an artillerist in any country," and "the victory was partially credited to the 'skill and gallantry' of Randolph's Howitzers."[13]

It was Magruder, however, who was accorded most of the glory for the Big Bethel victory. President Jefferson Davis announced the battle to be a "glorious victory."[14] While Robert E. Lee took pleasure in expressing "my gratification at the gallant conduct of the men under your command and approbation of the dispositions made by you, resulting as they did, in the rout of the enemy,"[15] Magruder was lauded by all for his leadership during the battle. On 12 June, the *Richmond Whig* reported that "during the entire

Private Richard Curtis, Wythe Rifles, 1861. *Courtesy of The Museum of the Confederacy.*

conflict, [Magruder's] voice was heard above the roar of cannon and musketry, and had the effect of magic on the men."[16] Two days later, the *Whig* stated that "during the entire engagement, Colonel Magruder was in every part of the field, and, displaying consummate generalship and courage, directing every movement in person and exposing himself with a recklessness of danger which was seen and admired by all in camp."[17] Female diarists added to the acclaim. Mary Boykin Chesnut of South Carolina wrote, "Colonel Magruder had done something splendid on the Peninsula,"[18] and from Richmond, Sallie Putman wrote that Prince John "calmly smoked his cigar and gave orders with coolness and deliberation."[19]

Legends even arose lauding Magruder's noble conduct following the battle. The Federals had retreated so rapidly from the battlefield that many of the dead and wounded were left behind. Magruder had the enemy dead buried and gave the wounded medical attention. On 11 June, Butler sent a detachment to recover these casualties. A Massachusetts soldier named Drake recounted the experience:

Our wounded that were left in that murderous affair at Bethel were by the enemy sent to Yorktown and well cared for. Our dead they decently buried not even so much as taking from their persons the least thing. I know this to be true because…we dug them up. One man had in his pocket quite a sum of gold…Colonel Magruder the secession commander of Bethel Forces gave us a good dinner, the best I have had since I left Boston and sent by us word to our commander that he was ready for us if we desired to attack him and that he should send as many of us to bloody graves as he was able to do.[20]

Magruder was reported to have said, under a flag of truce, to coordinate the return of Major Winthrop's body. Winthrop had already been given a military funeral, as many of the Confederates recognized that Major Winthrop, according to D.H. Hill, was the "only one of the enemy who exhibited an approximation of courage that day."[21] Winthrop's personal effects were returned. When the interview was over, Magruder had shaken hands with the young lieutenant on this solemn mission and said, "We part as friends, but on the field of battle we meet as enemies."[22]

Entrenchments at Big Bethel, 1862. *Courtesy of John Moran Quarstein.*

Despite his genteel actions over the recovery of Union casualties, Prince John soon found himself engaged in a war of words with General Butler. Magruder had learned that the Federals had captured four Confederates: one cavalry picket and three armed civilians. The opposing commanders exchanged pointed correspondence concerning a Private Carter who had been asleep when captured. Butler advised Magruder that Carter "was asleep at his post, and he informs me that his three companions left in such haste that they neglected to wake him up, and, they being mounted and my men on foot, the race was not a difficult one."[23] Prince John replied with his usual flair, "With respect to the vidette Private Carter, I desire to inform you that when a picket of four is placed out for twenty-four hours, as in this case, at least one is permitted to sleep. This picket had orders to retreat before a large force of the enemy. Four men against five thousand constituted, however, such great odds, as to have justified the retreat of the picket even without orders." Magruder concluded that had "Private Carter been awake, perhaps a retreat would not have been necessary."[24]

Even though Private Carter was exchanged, the two generals also argued about the three civilians who were captured during the early morning of 10 June. Butler stated that two of the civilians were armed when captured and the other, a Mr. Whiting, had fired on Federal soldiers. This circumstance, in Butler's mind, made them either soldiers or assassins. Magruder retorted, "The citizens in your possession are men who doubtless defended their homes against a foe who to their certain knowledge had with or without the authority of the Federal government destroyed that private property of their neighbors, breaking up even the pianos of the ladies and committing depredations numberless and of every description."[25]

While Butler admitted to Magruder "that there have been too many sporadic acts of wrong to private property committed by bad men under my Command," he added that the Confederate cavalry had fired into an ambulance during the Federal retreat: "My men complain that the ambulance having the wounded was fired into by your cavalry and I am informed that if you have any prisoners they were taken while in the pious duty to their wounded comrades and not in battle. It has never occurred to my mind that either firing into the ambulance or capturing persons in charge of the wounded was an act authorized, recognized, or sanctioned by any gentleman."[26]

Of course, Magruder replied with equal venom, claiming that no Confederate cavalry shot into an ambulance because the Federal retreat was too rapid for them to get ahead of the Union soldiers fleeing toward Newmarket Creek Bridge. He also defended the Virginia citizens as being "brave men, defending their firesides against piratical invasion, and are entitled to the respect of all good men."[27] Eventually, the civilians were exchanged.

Major General John Bankhead Magruder. *Courtesy of The Casemate Museum.*

The Southern press, upon learning about this exchange between the opposing commanders, believed that Magruder had won another victory equal to Big Bethel. It was even rumored that Prince John had challenged Butler to a duel to settle the matter in a gentlemanly manner. Southern newspapers rejoiced over Magruder's every comment as they typified his reputation as "the picture of the Virginia gentleman, the frank, manly representative of the chivalry of the dear Old Dominion."[28] Magruder was placed in the pantheon of Southern heroes with P.G.T. Beauregard and called "every inch a King."[29] "He's the hero for our times," one ballad proclaimed, "the furious fighting Johnny B. Magruder."[30] Exactly one week following the battle, 17 June 1861, Magruder was promoted to brigadier general. The fame seemed to fall upon Magruder naturally, and in every fashion he strove to live up to the honor bestowed upon him. He was a vigorous fifty-one years old, tall, erect and handsome. Always perfectly uniformed, he appeared magnificently everywhere at a gallop, talking incessantly despite his unusual lisp. His impressive nature, dramatic flair and strategic sense had given the South its first victory on the field of battle.

Big Bethel was a complete failure for the Union, and the Northern newspapers were harsh critics. One song was written to the tune of "Yankee Doodle" that epitomized this humiliating Union defeat:

> Butler and I went out to camp
> At Bethel to make a battle
> And then the Southerns whip't us back
> Just like a drove of cattle.
> Come though your swords and muskets drawn
> You do not find them handy
> Although the Yankees cannot fight
> At running, they're the dandy.[31]

Humiliation was felt throughout the North, even though many of the Union officers involved in the fight endeavored to lessen the engagement's impact. Colonel Joseph Carr of the 2nd New York Volunteers believed the "disastrous fight at Big Bethel" was of no importance. Carr considered Bethel a "battle we may scarce term it." The future major general believed that neither the Union officers nor men were prepared to conduct such an operation: "To the want of that experience and confidence a great measure of the failure at Big Bethel may be attributed," Carr commented. "Save as an encouragement to the Confederates," Carr concluded, Big Bethel "had no important result."[32]

Nevertheless, the Union ineptitude during the engagement required that a scapegoat be found. Butler was blamed for ordering his troops into battle with poor intelligence and for remaining at Fort Monroe during the battle. Gouverneur Warren later reported to the congressional committee on the conduct of the war that the plan was "from the very beginning evolved like a failure." Warren noted that the maps, which dated from 1819, were all wrong. The complicated advance "was planned for a night attack with very new troops, some of them had never been taught even to load and fire." Warren added, "To proceed from two different points, distant from each other six or seven miles."[33] The planning was poor, the leadership abysmal.

Of course, Butler strove to deflect all of the criticism away from himself. His confirmation as a major general of volunteers was at risk due to the public outcry. "Yet while no blame could seem to attach to me," Butler later wrote, "a senseless cry went out against me, and it almost lost me my

Lieutenant Colonel G.K. Warren,
5th New York Volunteer Regiment,
circa 1863. *Courtesy of the Schroeder
Collection.*

confirmation in the Senate." Butler blamed it all on Ebenezer Peirce. He noted that no one had criticized the plan when it was developed and that he had no choice but to place the strike against Big Bethel under the command of his senior brigadier general. "Everything was mismanaged," he lamented, "once the Union soldiers arrived upon the battlefield."[34]

> *From that time there did not seem to be a head more than a cabbage head to undertake to do anything, except it might be Winthrop. Greble held his position an hour and a half, while the main body of the troops stood about a half mile from his position waiting for the officers to form a plan of battle. They carefully disobeyed orders, which were…to go right ahead with fixed bayonets and fire but one shot, and they did not even do that. If they had only marched steadily forward…the enemy would have fled.*[35]

While Butler conceded that the plan evolved upon the battlefield, he maintained that the various efforts to strike at the Confederates were generally uncoordinated and disorganized. Once Winthrop was killed, Peirce held a "Council of Colonels," and all but Duryee considered retreat as the best course of action. Duryee, however, had already advised Peirce that his men were exhausted and should be withdrawn from the engagement. The overall justification was that the men had marched a long way and were hungry.

Peirce endeavored to organize a rear guard and an orderly retreat. It was all to no avail. As General Peirce later reported, "Some difficulty was experienced in keeping the men in proper order during the retreat, the men being so exhausted by thirst as to rush out of the ranks whenever water was to be had."[36]

Obviously, Ebenezer Peirce received most of the blame for the Union disaster. He was confused during much of the entire operation, and as a result, Captain Charles G. Bartlett of Duryee's Zouaves noted "there seemed to be no uniformity of action anywhere."[37] Zouave Karl Ahrendt witnessed during the battle Peirce "hiding behind a tree shivering with fright." Ahrendt believed that Peirce was a "slack and decrepit individual who would be far better suited for enjoying the comforts of a house and garden than leading a soldier's life."[38] Peter Washburn later wrote about the lack of battlefield leadership:

> We had no head...All the different commanders behaved nobly: but there was no reconnaissance, no plan of attack, and no concert of action. Hence the enemy were left to concentrate their whole force first against the Zouaves, then against Townsend's regiment, then against my men. A little military skill in the General, a little regard to the simplest rules of attack, would have rendered our charge successful. As it was, it was a failure—an egregious blunder.[39]

Peirce never regained control of his command following the friendly fire incident en route to Big Bethel. Most of his regimental commanders thought that the advance should have been cancelled following that deadly mistake; however, Peirce took the advice of Theodore Winthrop and followed Butler's orders to march on to engage the Confederates at Big Bethel. Several would later criticize this decision. Many of the officers and men were rather "skitterish" after the skirmish between the 3rd and 7th New York Regiments. Peirce was labeled incompetent and mustered out of the army after his ninety-day enlistment expired.

Despite the poor Union leadership and overly ambitious and ill-conceived plan, there were many who deserved acclaim during the battle. The Northern press tried to salvage some honor out of the defeat. The *New York Times* called the Union troops courageous as "they fought both friend and foe alike with equal resolution and only retired after exhausting their ammunition in the face of a powerful enemy." The friendly fire incident prompted a brief debate in the New York newspapers as to who was to blame for this deadly mistake. Both Townsend and Bendix were taken to task for not using an advance guard or skirmishes when operating in enemy territory. Louis Schaffner, the adjutant of the 7th New York, believed that several units in the 3rd New York wore uniforms similar to the enemy and caused the confusion. Furthermore, Schaffner noted that the mounted commanders and staff, as well as the failure to inform the Steuben Regiment about the white arm bands or password, caused the New Yorkers to fire into the compatriots. Some of the participants

Captain Charles Bartlett, 5th New York, 1864. *Courtesy of the Pohanka Collection.*

even questioned which regiment fired first. The debate ended with the recognition that it was a misfortunate affair; however, both Bendix and Townsend had done their duty when operating in enemy territory.

Some soldiers complained about their weapons. Most of the volunteer regiments were armed with older smoothbores. The Duryee's Zouaves were primarily equipped with outdated Model 1842 muskets that had limited range and accuracy. Sergeant Hart of the 5th New York lamented that "our miserable muskets will not carry…they are almost worthless."[40] Most of the Confederates were also armed with smoothbore muskets. Lieutenant Samuel Chisman's detachment from the Wythe Rifles was the only exception. Chisman's men carried Model 1855 Rifled Muskets.

While the soldiers and newspapers lauded the work of several regiments and individuals at Big Bethel, Theodore Winthrop and John T. Greble were lionized for their valor and sacrifice. Winthrop, who was told by Butler to "Be bold! Be bold! But not too bold,"[41] almost won the day for the Union with his bravery. Several articles he had penned about his service in Virginia were posthumously published by the *Atlantic Monthly*, which earned Winthrop even greater fame for his fateful heroism at Big Bethel.

Other officers and men received accolades for their devotion to duty at Big Bethel. Peirce made special reference "to the gallant and soldier-like conduct of Colonel Townsend, who was indefatigable in encouraging his men and leading them in the hottest scenes of the action."[42] He also noted that "Colonel Carr, in covering the retreat, showed himself a good soldier, ready and willing to do his duty."[43] G.K. Warren was also commended for remaining on the battlefield and recovering the dead and wounded directly after the battle. Captain Judson Kilpatrick of Duryee's Zouaves attained virtual hero status for his involvement in the engagement. He believed that the Zouaves' advance on the one-gun battery almost brought the Union success, as he wrote, "Captains Winslow, Bartlett, and myself charged with our commands in front. The enemy was forced out of the first battery, all the forces were rapidly advancing…everything promised a speedy victory. Where this order came from I do not know."[43] He concluded his report by giving laurels to others:

> *It gives me great pleasure to mention the gallant conduct of Captain Bartlett, who came up with the reserve, re-enforcing my line, and was ever at the point of danger encouraging his men. Lieutenant York, in command of my left, and Lieutenant Churchill J. Cambrelling, in command at my right, displayed the greatest bravery. Lieutenant York's sword was broken by a grape shot, and he was slightly wounded in the leg. I shall ever be grateful to Captain Winslow, who rescued me after our forces had left. He came to my aid, assisted by Sergeants Orderdonk and Angus. At the last moment but in time to rescue me from the enemy. I would also favorably mention Private Wood, who brought me valuable information, and who fired the first shot; Private John Dunn, whose arm was shattered by a cannon ball, and who bore himself with the greatest bravery, and who said to Surgeon Rufus H. Gilbert, while amputating his arm, which he could not have lost it in a nobler cause. The whole command, men and officers, did themselves the greatest credit, and I am satisfied can conquer anything except impossibilities.*[44]

Lieutenant Churchill J.
Cambrelling, 5ᵗʰ New York, 1861.
Courtesy of the Schroeder Collection.

Big Bethel was filled with difficulties and impossibilities for the Union. Despite the individual bravery, the Federal plan and execution could not overwhelm the superior Confederate leadership, élan and defensive preparations.

Big Bethel had major consequences for the Union and Confederate forces on the Peninsula. During the next ten months, the Federals were content to control the very tip of the Peninsula below Newmarket Creek. The Union was able to use this position to protect the lower Chesapeake Bay as a base for the North Atlantic Blockading Squadron. Fort Monroe guarded the Hampton Roads harbor and allowed the Federals to use the anchorage for amphibious operations against Hatteras Inlet, Port Royal Sound, Roanoke Island and New Orleans. Furthermore, the Union-controlled Lower Peninsula enabled the Union to welcome more escaped slaves as contraband of war. Contraband communities and schools were created and thrived. The Confederates, despite Magruder's wish to sweep the Federals into the sea, were unable to contest the Union Department of Virginia's control of the Virginia Peninsula's tip. This circumstance would cause the burning of Hampton on 7 August 1861 and the use of Fort Monroe as a base for McClellan's 1862 Peninsula Campaign strike against Richmond.

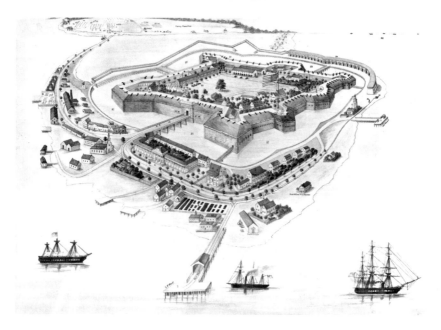

Fortress Monroe, February 1862. *Courtesy of John Moran Quarstein.*

The Confederate victory at Big Bethel, nevertheless, blocked the first Union advance against Richmond via the Peninsula. The battle lines were drawn, and the Confederates maintained control of the Peninsula north of Brick Kiln Creek. The area between the northwest and southwest branches of the Back River became a no-man's land. This strategic situation allowed the Confederates to construct an in-depth defensive system that would eventually befuddle Major General George B. McClellan during the early stages of his 1862 Peninsula Campaign. Magruder's ability to retain control of the Peninsula protected the industrial centers of Norfolk and Portsmouth and allowed the Confederates to create their ironclad, the CSS *Virginia*. Furthermore, it enabled the Confederates to use this rich agricultural region to gather much-needed food and supplies.

On the national scene, Big Bethel would eventually fade in importance. Even though it would retain its status as the war's first land battle, it was merely a skirmish and would be overshadowed by bloody and decisive battles such as First Manassas and Shiloh. Nevertheless, Bethel had a major impact on both sides. Ben Butler reported after the battle to Winfield Scott, "I think, the unfortunate combination of circumstances and the result

Sergeant Edward George Bell,
5th New York, 1861. *Courtesy of the
Schroeder Collection.*

which were experienced, we have gained more than we lost. Our troops
have learned to have confidence in themselves under fire…Our officers have
learned wherein their organization and drill are inefficient."[45] The Union
men who were at Big Bethel gained battlefield experience and a recognition
that it would require a serious commitment to ensure that the Union would
be preserved. One unidentified New Yorker wrote, "I have seen enough to
satisfy me that warfare ain't play."[46]

In turn, the Confederate victory at Big Bethel raised enthusiasm for the
war and reinforced the myth that one Southerner could defeat at least four or
five Northerners. Consequently, they felt that they could indeed win the war.
The Confederates believed that their victory would prompt the Northern
"moneyed men" to recognize that the war could not be won and that peace
should be made. On 17 June 1861, the *Richmond Dispatch* summed up this
attitude when it published that Big Bethel

is one of the most extraordinary victories in the annals of war. Four thousand thoroughly drilled and equipped troops routed and driven from the field by only eleven hundred men…does not the hand of God seem manifest in this thing? The courage and conduct of the noble sons of the South engaged in this battle are beyond all praise. They have crowned the name of their country with imperishable luster and made their own names immortal with odds of four to one against them, they have achieved a complete victory, putting their enemy to inglorious flight, and giving to the world a brilliant pledge of the manner in which the South can defend its firesides and altars.[47]

Other newspapers chimed in with their praise. The *Richmond Whig* proclaimed, "The rush, the dash, the élan of our boys was, however, the great and distinguishing feature of the affair…Their dashing bearing, in the face of four times their number, will inspire a spirit of emulation among all our forces, and lead to the rout of the invaders wherever they show themselves."[48] The *Petersburg Express* lauded all "in this first pitched battle on Virginia soil in behalf of Southern rights and independence."[49]

While many believed that the Confederate victory justified the correctness of secession or the superiority of the Southern soldier, the staunch Presbyterian and one of the true heroes of Big Bethel wrote his wife that it all was simply due to God's will. "I have to thank God for a great and decided victory and that I have escaped with a slight contusion of the knee," Hill reflected. "It is a little singular that my first battle in this war should be at Bethel where I was baptized and worshipped until I was sixteen years old, the church of my mother. Was she not a guardian spirit in the battle, averting ball and shell? Oh, God, give me gratitude to Thee, and may we never dishonor Thee by weak faith!"[50]

Despite all the detailed press coverage in both the North and South, Big Bethel would quickly become a minor memory. Almost six thousand men were part of the engagement. Some of these men would go on to greater acclaim, and others would serve their enlistments and return home. All of them would never forget their first baptism of fire that hot day at Big Bethel Church.

Nor shall glory be forgot
While fame her record keeps
Or where honor points the hallowed ground
Where valor proudly sleeps.[51]

Appendix I

Order of Battle

UNION

Brigadier General Ebenezer Peirce, 4,400 men
1st New York—Colonel William Allen, 750 men
2nd New York—Colonel Joseph B. Carr, 750 men
3rd New York—Colonel Frederick Townsend, 650 men
5th New York—Colonel Abram Duryee, 850 men
7th New York—Colonel John Bendix, 750 men
4th Massachusetts—Major Horace O. Wittemore, 300 men
1st Vermont—Lieutenant Colonel Peter Washburn, 300 men
2nd U.S. Artillery—Lieutenant John Trout Greble, 50 men

CONFEDERATE

Colonel John Bankhead Magruder, 1,404 men
1st North Carolina—Colonel D.H. Hill, 800 men
    Edgecombe Guards—Captain John L. Bridgers
    Hornets Nest Rifles—Captain Lewis S. Williams
    Charlotte Greys—Captain Egbert Ross
    Orange Light Infantry—Captain Richard J. Ashe
    Buncombe Riflemen—Captain W.W. McDowell

La Fayette Light Infantry—Captain Joseph B. Starr
Burke Rifles—Captain Clark M. Avery
Fayetteville Independent Light Infantry—Captain W. Huske
Enfield Blues—Captain David B. Bell
Southern Stars—Captain W.J. Hoke
3rd Virginia—Lieutenant Colonel William Stuart, 208 men
    Young Guard—Captain William H. Charters
    Southern Guard—Captain Jackson F. Childrey
    Virginia Life Guard—Captain John S. Walker
Virginia Battalion—Major Edgar B. Montague, 140 men
    Halifax Light Infantry—Captain John Grammer Jr.
    Chatham Grays—Captain William H. Werth
    Old Dominion Riflemen—Captain Henry D. Dickerson
Army of the Peninsula Cavalry—Major John Bell Hood, 100 men (later to become 3rd Virginia Cavalry)
    Charles City Light Dragoons—Captain Robert Douthatt
    Old Dominion Dragoons—Captain Jefferson Curle Phillips
Mecklenburg Dragoons—Captain William N. Jones
Wythe Rifles—Lieutenant Samuel R. Chisman, 28 men
Richmond Howitzers—Major George Wythe Randolph, 150 men
    2nd Company—Lieutenant John Thompson Brown
    3rd Company—Captain Robert Conway Stanard

Appendix II

First Battle

The Civil War featured many firsts in American history. Balloon launchings, ironclads and railroads can fill books with pages of facts, interpretations and illustrations. Where or when several of these firsts occurred are thoroughly discussed, particularly when the first battle took place. Big Bethel is generally considered the first land battle of the war. Nevertheless, this first is often heartily debated.

Webster's Collegiate Dictionary has several definitions of the word "battle." The primary is "battle implies a general and prolonged combat" or "a general encounter between armies, ships of war, or airplanes." This definition does not clarify how to classify the war's first battle. If we understand the differences between words like bombardment (to attack with artillery), riot (a tumultuous disturbance of the public peace by three or more persons assembled together and acting with common intent), engagement (a hostile encounter between military forces) and combat (to fight with or to struggle against), these terms do not bring a complete answer; however, the meaning of these words will help understand what constitutes the Civil War's first battle.

The first shots of the Civil War happened in Charleston Harbor, 12–14 April 1861. This thirty-four-hour bombardment witnessed no casualties (Private Hough, the first soldier to die during the war, was accidentally killed as the Union soldiers fired a one-hundred-gun salute as they evacuated the fort) and was an artillery exchange. Soldiers did not face one another on an open battlefield.

The 19 April 1861 Baltimore Riot witnessed the first casualties caused by gunfire. Nevertheless, the 6th Massachusetts soldiers were mobbed by civilians as they marched from Union Station down Pratt Street to Camden Yards. Four militiamen and twelve civilians were killed. Since the Baltimoreans were an unorganized mob, they do not meet the definition of an armed and trained force operating under a central command. Thus, the Baltimore Riot cannot be considered a battle.

The next gunfire was heard at Sewell's Point. Virginia Militia Major General Walter Gwynn, an 1822 West Point graduate, organized the construction of fortifications guarding the entrance to the Elizabeth River. The Confederates had recently captured Gosport Navy Yard and used some of the heavy cannon abandoned by the Federals to arm the newly built batteries. On 18 May 1861, the steamer USS *Monticello*, commanded by Lieutenant D.L. Braine, shelled the Confederate fortifications. Braine returned the next day with his ship and another gunboat, USS *Stepping Stones*, and exchanged cannon fire with the Confederate defenses. The bombardment had no recorded casualties. Consequently, the action at Sewell's Point cannot be considered a battle, as it was just an artillery exchange with no injuries.

On 1 June 1861, a skirmish occurred at Fairfax Court House. In the predawn hours, fifty men of Company B, 2nd U.S. Cavalry, commanded by Lieutenant Charles H. Tompkins, rode into town firing their weapons. The Warrenton Rifles quickly mustered. As they were unable to locate their commander, Captain John Quincy Marr, two officers—former Virginia Governor Colonel William "Extra Billy" Smith and Lieutenant Colonel Richard Stoddard Ewell—organized the men. They returned a volley as the Union cavalrymen rode out of town. The Federals reported capturing five Confederates and suffered themselves four wounded and lost nine horses. The "skirmish," as Ewell referred to the encounter, was over in minutes. The Confederates incurred three casualties, one killed and two wounded. West Point graduate R.S. Ewell received a fresh wound in the shoulder, and a member of the Warrenton Rifles was struck in the breast by a spent ball. Unfortunately, the Confederate killed during this engagement was VMI graduate and prewar lawyer Captain John Quincy Marr. Marr was discovered after daylight, eight hundred feet southwest of the courthouse, dead in a field of clover. He had been killed by a stray bullet and was the first

Confederate officer killed in the war. The skirmish at Fairfax Court House was a brief encounter, more of a raid than a standup battle. None of the official reports submitted by the participants refer to the incident as a battle.

The one engagement that might be considered a battle was the minor action at Philippi, West Virginia, on 3 June 1861. A Confederate force of 1,500 hundred men, under the command of Colonel George A. Porterfield, was surprised in their sleep when Federal artillery opened fire on the town at dawn. Porterfield's men simply ran away and did not contest the Union advance. The Federals referred to this minor action as the "Philippi Races." The Federals suffered 2 wounded and the Confederates 15 wounded. The Confederate injured were left behind, including Private James Hangar, who lost his leg to a cannonball and became the war's first amputee.

Philippi should not challenge Big Bethel as the war's first battle, as the Confederates ran away from the field without organizing a resistance to the Union concentric night attack. No one was killed. At Big Bethel, two opposing forces arrived on the battlefield and fought for over three hours in a sustained effort to control the crossing of Brick Kiln Creek. The Federals suffered eighteen killed and fifty-eight wounded. The Confederates had ten casualties. Henry Lawson Wyatt was their only fatality. Both armies stood and fired volley after volley at their enemies. The Confederate use of field fortifications enabled their 1,400 defenders to repel the piecemeal attacks of the Federal 4,400-strong strike force. While the engagement is rightly considered a skirmish in comparison to the later large battles, Big Bethel is, indeed, the first land battle of the Civil War.

Casualties

CONFEDERATE

REGIMENT	KILLED	WOUNDED	MISSING	TOTAL
1st North Carolina	1	6	-	7
Richmond Howitzers	-	3	-	3
Total	1	9	-	10

UNION

REGIMENT	KILLED	WOUNDED	MISSING	TOTAL
Staff	1	-	-	1
4th Massachusetts	1	-	-	1
1st New York	2	1	-	3
2nd New York	-	2	1	3
3rd New York	2	27	1	30
5th New York	6	13	-	19
7th New York	3	7	2	12
1st Vermont	2	3	1	6
2nd U.S. Artillery	1	-	-	1
Total	18	53	5	76

Bethel: A Proving Ground for Generals

Big Bethel was a baptism of fire for the Union and Confederate soldiers who served in the engagement. Several officers would rise beyond many expectations during the struggle that followed the battle.

John Bankhead Magruder was the first to be promoted. On 17 June 1861, he was named brigadier general and then promoted major general on 7 October 1861. Magruder retained his command on the Peninsula and eventually constructed three defensive lines defending this approach against Richmond. Magruder once again attained hero status as his thirteen-thousand-man command blocked Major General George B. McClellan's advance for almost a month during the early stages of the 1862 Peninsula Campaign. Although he was lauded for his bluff during the engagement at Oak Grove, the first of the Seven Days Battles, he appeared cautious and confused at Savage Station and Malvern Hill. Magruder was reassigned as commander of the Department of Texas and again flashed his brilliance with the capture of Galveston on 1 January 1863. He remained in Texas until the war's end.

Daniel Harvey Hill was also promoted, on 10 July 1861, brigadier general for his conspicuous service at Big Bethel. He was named major general on 26 March 1862. He served during the Peninsula and Antietam Campaigns. Sent to North Carolina to organize the defenses of that state, he returned to Virginia to defend Richmond during the Gettysburg Campaign. Hill was promoted lieutenant general and sent to the Army of Tennessee. He fought well at Chickamauga; however, when he recommended the removal of Braxton Bragg on grounds of incompetence, he ran afoul of President Jefferson Davis, and his lieutenant general's appointment was not confirmed. He did not have another command until March 1865 at Bentonville.

Another officer at Big Bethel to attain the rank of lieutenant general was John Bell Hood. Hood received command of the Texas Brigade with the rank of brigadier general on 26 March 1862. He quickly became a divisional commander and major general in Longstreet's Corps. Badly wounded at Gettysburg, he went to fight at Chickamauga, where he was wounded again. Hood's right leg was amputated at the hip. Promoted lieutenant general, Hood served under General Joe Johnston in the Army of Tennessee. Hood was promoted full general and replaced Johnston; however, his leadership was not up to the task. He failed to save Atlanta or to recapture Nashville.

Robert Hoke, a second lieutenant in the 1st North Carolina at Big Bethel, attained two stars. He assumed command of Trimble's Brigade at Fredericksburg in December 1862 and was promoted brigadier general one month later. Hoke was badly wounded at Chancellorsville; however, his brilliant performance capturing Plymouth, North Carolina, on 20 April 1864 resulted in his promotion to major general. He also served at Bermuda Hundred, Cold Harbor and the battles around Petersburg and Bentonville, North Carolina.

Three other Confederate officers at Bethel would achieve the rank of brigadier general. James Henry Lane commanded a brigade in the Army of Northern Virginia from Antietam to Appomattox. William Gaston Lewis was a lieutenant in the Edgecombe Guards at Big Bethel and would rise in rank until he was named brigadier general on 31 May 1864. He was severely wounded and captured near Farmville, Virginia, on 7 April 1865. George Wythe Randolph was promoted brigadier general on 12 February 1862; however, he was appointed secretary of war on 22 March 1862. He served in this position until 15 November 1862, when he resigned to take the field again. Randolph's poor health (he suffered from tuberculosis) forced him to resign his commission in 1864.

The Federals also witnessed Big Bethel as an incubator for generalship. While Peirce lost his brigadier general commission, he sought to redeem himself and enlisted as a private. He was eventually appointed regimental commander of the 29th Massachusetts. He lost an arm at White Oak Swamp on 30 June 1862 and resigned his commission in November 1862. John

Bendix eventually became colonel of the 10th New York and was mustered out of the service on 7 May 1863. Nevertheless, when the conflict ended, he was brevetted brigadier general for "war service." Frederick Townsend also was brevetted for war service; however, he served most of the war (1863–66) as acting assistant provost marshal of New York State. He resigned his commission as lieutenant colonel of the 9th U.S. Infantry in 1868.

Benjamin Franklin Butler had his major general appointment confirmed. He left the Union Department of Virginia to command the troops involved in the capture of Hatteras Inlet, 29 August 1861. He recruited an amphibious division and commanded it during the capture of New Orleans. A capable military governor, he aroused passions in the South, North and overseas due to his decisions such as his "Woman's Order" in New Orleans. He would become the only general during the war to have his likeness mass produced on the bottom of a chamber pot. He was nicknamed "Beast" for his governorship of New Orleans and "Spoons" for allegedly stealing silver from Southern homes. He returned to Virginia and eventually became the commander of the Army of the James. Despite his military incompetence, his political influence forced President Lincoln to retain him in command until the failed Fort Fisher expedition in December 1864, after which he was sacked.

Abram Duryee was promoted brigadier general and commanded a brigade until 30 January 1863, when he resigned. Duryee was wounded three times during the Antietam Campaign. Another member of the 5th New York to earn a star was Henry Eugene Davies. A graduate of Columbia University, Davies served after Bethel in Judson Kilpatrick's 2nd U.S. Cavalry. He was promoted brigadier general on 16 September 1863. He assumed command of 2nd Division, Army of the Potomac Cavalry Corps, in September 1864. Davies led his division with distinction during the Petersburg and Appomattox Campaigns. He was promoted major general on 4 May 1865 and resigned in 1866 to resume his law practice. Joseph Carr was promoted brigadier general on 7 September 1862, spending most of the war in the Army of the Potomac. Carr was brevetted major for war service and became a major general in the New York State Militia after the war. After his service on the Peninsula, John Wolcott Phelps commanded the Ship Island Expedition and then served as a brigade commander during the capture of New Orleans. Once in New Orleans, he promoted the idea of recruiting African Americans for U.S. Army service. When his concept was rejected, he resigned on 21 August 1862. When news of Phelps's plan reached the Confederate government, he was declared an outlaw for organizing slaves for military service.

Judson Kilpatrick gained the fame he sought at Big Bethel. He was the first Regular Army officer wounded in action and was promoted lieutenant colonel with the 2nd U.S. Cavalry. Following the Battle of Second Manassas, he was given command of his unit and promoted colonel. Kilpatrick was promoted brigadier general in June 1863, following the Battle of Beverly Ford. He would be appointed commander of the 3rd Cavalry Division, Army of the Potomac, during the Gettysburg Campaign. He commanded an expedition destroying Confederate gunboats and shipping along the Rappahannock River and then the notorious Kilpatrick-Dahlgren Raid. General William T. Sherman requested that Kilpatrick join his command, stating, "I know Kilpatrick is a hell of a damned fool, but I want just that sort of man to command my cavalry on this expedition." He commanded Sherman's cavalry force during the March to the Sea and Carolina's Campaign. He was promoted major general on 18 June 1865 and later served as minister to Chile.

Gouverneur Kemble Warren perhaps achieved the greatest success of any of the Union officers at Big Bethel. He was promoted colonel and placed in command of the 5th New York and then a brigade. He successfully commanded his unit during the 1862 Peninsula Campaign through Fredericksburg. He was wounded at Gaines Mill and was appointed brigadier general. Warren was named chief topographical engineer for the Army of the Potomac and then its chief engineer on 8 June 1863. General Warren played a significant role on the second day at Gettysburg when he recognized the need to defend Little Round Top and successfully organized this position's defenses just as the Confederates launched their attack. He was wounded during this action. Warren was given command of the II Corps, and from March 1864 until 1 April 1865, he commanded the V Corps. He was relieved by General Phil Sheridan at Five Forks. Although he was exonerated of Sheridan's charges after a Court of Inquiry, Warren was professionally ruined. In 1882, it was said that he died of a "broken heart" as a result of this incident.

Notes

Chapter 1

1. *Richmond Daily Enquirer*, 22 April 1861.
2. *War of the Rebellion* (hereinafter cited as OR), Series I, Vol. II, 612.
3. Wallace, *The Richmond Howitzers*, 47.
4. Quarstein, *CSS* Virginia, 20.
5. Clark, *Histories of the Several Regiments*, 81.
6. Jensen, *32nd Virginia Infantry*, 11.
7. Ibid.

Chapter 2

1. Holzman, *Stormy Ben Butler*, 26.
2. Ibid., 30.
3. Ibid.
4. Ibid., 31.
5. Ibid., 33.
6. Nolan, *Benjamin Franklin Butler*, 31.
7. Ibid., 35.
8. Holzman, *Stormy Ben Butler*, 39.
9. Ibid., 42.

10. Ibid.

11. Ibid., 44.

12. Ibid., 45.

13. Ibid.

14. Ibid., 48.

15. Ibid., 49.

16. Ibid.

17. OR, Series I, Vol. 2, 37.

18. Holzman, *Stormy Ben Butler*, 45.

19. Ibid., 47.

20. *London Times*, 16 May 1861.

21. Holzman, *Stormy Ben Butler*, 47.

22. OR, Series I, Vol. 2, 817.

23. Unidentified, "Recollections of Cadet Life," *Army and Navy Journal* 4 (3 August 1867): 794.

24. Benjamin Stoddert Ewell Papers.

25. Lee, *Memoirs of William Nelson Pendleton*, 27.

26. Monroe and McIntosh, *Papers of Jefferson Davis*, 73.

27. "Ebbett," "John Magruder," *Army and Navy Journal* (25 September 1880): 148.

28. Casdorph, *Prince John Magruder*, 30.

29. Ibid., 49.

30. Ibid., 148.

31. U.S. Congress, Senate I (1848), 263.

32. Cooke, *Stonewall Jackson*, 14–15.

33. George Ballentine, *Autobiography of an English Soldier*, 215.

34. William Booth Taliaferro Papers.

35. Stewart, *John Phoenix, Esq.*, 53.

36. Casdorph, *Prince John Magruder*, 81.

37. Haskin, *History*, 321.

38. White, "Founder of Fort Yuma," 137.

39. Casdorph, *Prince John Magruder*, 87.

40. White, "Founder of Fort Yuma," 137.

41. Casdorph, *Prince John Magruder*, 96.

42. Long, "Memoir of General John Bankhead Magruder," 105.

43. Ibid.

44. *History of the State of Kansas*, 418.

45. Long, "Memoir of General John Bankhead Magruder," 106.

46. Ibid.

47. *New York Times*, 23 May 1870.

48. Hale, *Four Valiant Years*, 247.

49. Casdorph, *Prince John Magruder*, 269.

50. Freeman, *Lee's Lieutenants*, Vol. I, XXXN.

CHAPTER 3

1. OR, Series I, Vol. 2, 640–41.

2. Benedict, *Vermont in the Civil War*, 28.

3. Ibid., 33.

4. *New York Herald*, 11 May 1861.

5. Benedict, *Vermont in the Civil War*, 36.

6. Jensen, *32nd Virginia Infantry*, 16–17.

7. OR, Series I, Vol. 2, 297–98.

8. Ibid.

9. Ibid.

10. Ibid., 54.

11. Osborne, *History of the Twenty-ninth Regiment of Massachusetts*, 60.

12. Delafield, Mordecai and McClellan, *Report Published by Secretary of War*, 207.

13. Hunter, "Butler Zouaves."

14. Ibid.

15. Ibid.

16. Ibid.

17. *New York Times*, 1 May 1861.

18. Carr, "Operations of 1861 About Fort Monroe," 145.

19. OR, Series 1, Vol. 2, 37.

20. Ibid., 38.

21. Ibid.

22. Ibid., 870–71.

23. Ibid., 888.

24. Pohanka, "Red-legged Devils."

25. Rouse, *When the Yankees Came*, 64.

26. Bridger, *Lee's Maverick General*, 17.

CHAPTER 4

1. Barefoot, *General Robert F. Hoke*, 26.

2. *New York Herald*, 12 June 1861.

3. Pohanka, "Red-legged Devils."

4. Carr, "Operations of 1861 About Fort Monroe," 149.

5. *New York Times*, 6 June 1861.

6. Pohanka, "Red-legged Devils."

7. Carr, "Operations of 1861 About Fort Monroe," 151.

8. Pohanka, "Red-legged Devils."

9. U.S. Department of the Navy, *Official Records of the Union and Confederate Navies in the War of the Rebellion*, Series 2, Vol. 2, 113.

10. Bridger, *Lee's Maverick General*, 29.

11. OR, Series I, Vol. 2, 93.

12. Wellman, *Rebel Boast*, 49.

13. Ratchford, *Some Reminiscences*, 13.

14. Barefoot, *General Robert F. Hoke*, 28.

15. OR, Series I, Vol. 2, 93.

16. *North Carolina Whig*, 18 June 1861.

17. Wellman, *Rebel Boast*, 50.

18. OR, Series I, Vol. 2, 93.

19. Lee, "Magruder's Peninsula Campaign," 64.

20. Ibid.

21. Butler, *Butler's Book*, 267–68.

22. Ibid., 269.

CHAPTER 5

1. Davenport, *Camp and Field Life*, 56.

2. OR, Series I, Vol. 2, 87.

3. Ibid., 84.

4. Pohanka, "Red-legged Devils."

5. OR, Series I, Vol. 2, 84.

6. Ibid., 89.

7. White, *A Diary of the War*, 38.

8. Barefoot, *General Robert F. Hoke*, 31.

9. OR, Series I, Vol. 2, 88.

10. Huske, "Account of the Battle of Big Bethel."

11. Wellman, *Rebel Boast*, 52.

12. Pohanka, "Red-legged Devils."

13. Ibid.

14. Southwick, *A Duryee Zouave*, 42.

15. *Brooklyn Daily Eagle*, 1 July 1861.

16. Pohanka, "Red-legged Devils."

17. Ibid.

18. OR Series I, Vol. 2, 89.

19. Ibid.

20. Davenport, *Camp and Field Life*, 58.

21. OR, Series I, Vol. 51, pt. 1, 4.

22. Ibid., Vol. 2, 94.

23. Hord, "The Battle of Big Bethel, VA," 419.

24. OR, Series I, Vol. 2, 95.

25. Pohanka, "Red-legged Devils."

26. *Hillsborough Recorder*, 16 June 1861.

27. OR, Series I, Vol. 2, 94.

28. Ibid., 95.

29. Ibid., 87.

30. Ibid.

31. Clark, *Histories of the Several Regiments*, 101.

32. Pohanka, "Red-legged Devils."

33. Wellman, *Rebel Boast*, 54.

34. Huske, "Account of the Battle of Big Bethel."

35. OR, Series I, Vol. 2, 93.

36. Ibid., 99.

37. Ibid., 86.

38. Ibid., 92.

39. Ibid.

40. Pohanka, "Red-legged Devils."

41. *New York Times*, 14 June 1861.

42. *Richmond Dispatch*, 8 June 1861.

43. White, *A Diary of the War*, 26.

44. Wellman, *Rebel Boast*, 57.

45. OR, Series I, Vol. 2, 93.

46. Pohanka, "Red-legged Devils."

47. Southwick, 43.

48. Pohanka, "Red-legged Devils."

49. Ibid.

50. Davenport, *Camp and Field Life*, 60.

51. Pohanka, "Red-legged Devils."

52. Ibid.

Chapter 6

1. Huske, "Account of the Battle of Big Bethel."

2. Clark, *Histories of the Several Regiments*, 101; Woodward, *Mary Chesnut's Civil War*, 82.

3. Huske, "Account of the Battle of Big Bethel."

4. Ibid.

5. Chapman, *More Terrible than Victory*, 35.

6. Huske, "Account of the Battle of Big Bethel."

7. OR, Series I, Vol. 2, 95.

8. Hord, "The Battle of Big Bethel, VA," 420.

9. OR, Series I, Vol. 2, 93.

10. Ibid., 95.

11. Ibid., 93.

12. Clark, *Histories of the Several Regiments*, 102.

13. OR, Series I, Vol. 2, 94.

14. Ibid., 925.

15. Ibid., 103.

16. *Richmond Whig*, 12 June 1861.

17. Ibid., 14 June 1861.

18. Woodward, *Mary Chesnut's Civil War*.

19. *Richmond Dispatch*, 17 June 1861.

20. Loose clipping, Virginia War Museum.

21. OR, Series I, Vol. 2, 95.

22. *Richmond Dispatch*, 24 June 1861.

23. OR, Series I, Vol. 2, 682.

24. Ibid.

25. Ibid.

26. Ibid., 664.

27. Ibid., 683.

28. *Richmond Dispatch*, 26 June 1861.

29. Ibid., 10 July 1861.

30. Faust, *Historical Times Illustrated*, 468.

31. Virginia War Museum.

32. Carr, "Operations of 1861 About Fort Monroe," 151.

33. Report of the Joint Commission, 384.

34. Butler, *Butler's Book*, 269.

35. OR, Series I, Vol. 2, 86.

36. Ibid.

37. Pohanka, "Red-legged Devils."

38. Ibid.

39. Benedict, *Vermont in the Civil War*, 39.

40. Pohanka, "Red-legged Devils."

41. Butler, *Butler's Book*, 259.

42. OR, Series I, Vol. 2, 87.

43. Ibid.

44. Ibid., 90.

45. Ibid., 86.

46. *New York Leader*, 22 June 1861.

47. *Richmond Dispatch*, 17 June 1861.

48. *Richmond Whig*, 14 June 1861.

49. *Petersburg Express*, 12 June 1861.

50. Freeman, *Lee's Lieutenants*, 21.

51. Confederate Monument, Bentonville Battlefield, Bentonville, North Carolina.

Bibliography

Primary Sources

Ballentine, George. *Autobiography of an English Soldier in the United States Army Comprising Observations and Adventures in the United States and Mexico.* New York: Stringer and Townsend, 1853.

Benedict, G.G. *Vermont in the Civil War: A History of the Part Taken by the Vermont Soldiers and Sailors in the War of the Union 1861–65.* 2 vols. Burlington, VT: Free Press Association, 1886.

Butler, Benjamin F. *Butler's Book.* Boston: A.M. Thayer & Co., 1892.

Carr, Joseph B. "Operations of 1861 About Fort Monroe." In *Battles and Leaders of the Civil War.* 5 vols. Edited by Robert Underwood and Clarence Clough Buck. New York: Century Co., 1887.

Clark, Walker, ed. *Histories of the Several Regiments and Battalions from North Carolina in the Great War 1861–1865.* Raleigh, NC: E.M. Uzzell, Printer and Binder, 1901.

Cooke, John Esten. *Stonewall Jackson: A Military History.* New York: D. Appleton and Co., 1866.

Davenport, Alfred. *Camp and Field Life of the Fifth New York Infantry*. New York: Dick and Fitzgerald, 1879.

Delafield, Richard, Alfred Mordecai and George McClellan. *Report Published by Secretary of War of Military Commission to Europe*. 2 vols. Washington, D.C.: Government Printing Office, 1857–60.

Haskin, William L. *The History of the First Regiment of the Artillery from its Organization in 1821, to January 1ˢᵗ 1879*. Portland, ME: B. Thurston and Co., 1879.

History of the State of Kansas. Chicago: A.T. Andreas, 1883.

Hood, John Bell. *Advance and Retreat: Personal Experiences United States and Confederate Armies*. New Orleans, LA: Hood Orphan Memorial Fund, 1880.

Lee, Sarah P., ed. *Memoirs of William Nelson Pendleton, DD*. Philadelphia: J.B. Lippincott, 1893.

Monroe, Haskell M., and James T. McIntosh, eds. *The Papers of Jefferson Davis*. 3 vols. Baton Rouge: Louisiana State University Press, 1965.

Osborne, William H. *History of the Twenty-ninth Regiments of Massachusetts*. Boston, 1877.

Ratchford, J.W. *Some Reminiscences of Persons and Incidents of the Civil War*. Richmond, VA: Whittet and Shepperson, 1909.

Report of the Joint Commission on the Conduct of the War. Rep., Com. No. 108, 37ᵗʰ Congress, 3ʳᵈ sess. (1863). Part 3. Washington, D.C.: Government Printing Office.

Rouse, Parke, Jr. *When the Yankees Came*. Richmond, VA: Deetz Press, 1977.

Stewart, George R. *John Phoenix, Esq., the Veritable Squibob: A Life of Captain George H. Derby, USA*. New York: Da Capo Press (reprint), 1969.

U.S. Congress, Senate I (1848). Washington, D.C.: Government Printing Office, 1850.

War of the Rebellion: A Compilation of the Official Records of the Union and Confederate Armies. Washington, D.C.: Government Printing Office, 1880–1901.

White, William S. *A Diary of the War, Or What I Saw of It.* Richmond, VA, 1883.

Woodward, C. Vann, ed. *Mary Chesnut's Civil War.* New Haven, CT: Yale University Press, 1981.

Newspapers

Brooklyn Daily Eagle
Hillsborough Recorder
London Times
New York Herald
New York Leader
New York Times
North Carolina Whig
Petersburg Express
Richmond Daily Enquirer
Richmond Dispatch
San Antonio Light

Periodicals

Britton, Rick. "To War! Big Bethel: The Civil War's First Battle." *Command* 53 (n.d.).

Dinkens, James. "The Battle of Big Bethel, VA." *The Confederate Veteran Magazine* (1896).

Hord, B.M. "The Battle of Big Bethel, VA." *The Confederate Veteran Magazine* (1911).

King, Kendall J. "Bold, But Not Too Bold." *America's Civil War* 6, no. 1 (March 1993).

Lee, Baker. "Magruder's Peninsula Campaign in 1862." *Southern Historical Society Papers* (1892).

Long, Armistead. "Memoir of General John Bankhead Magruder." *Southern Historical Society Papers* 12 (1884).

Norris, David A. "The Lexington of the Civil War." *American History* 36, no. 4 (2001).

Unpublished Manuscripts and Dissertations

Benjamin Stoddert Ewell Papers. Earl Gregg Swem Library, College of William and Mary, Williamsburg, Virginia.

Big Bethel Papers. Virginia War Museum, Newport News, Virginia.

Hunter, Thomas A. "Butler Zouaves." Onondaga Historical Association, Syracuse, New York.

Huske, Benjamin. "Account of the Battle of Big Bethel." North Carolina Department of Archives and History (NCDAH).

Pohanka, Brian C. "Red-legged Devils: History of the Fifth New York Volunteer Infantry: Duryee's Zouaves." Archives. Unpublished manuscript.

White, Arthur. "Founder of Fort Yuma: Excerpts from the Diary of Major Samuel Heintzelman. USA, 1849–1852." Master's thesis, University of San Diego, 1975.

William Booth Taliaferro Papers. Earl Gregg Swem Library, College of William and Mary, Williamsburg, Virginia.

BOOKS

Arthur, Robert, and Richard P. Weinert Jr. *Defender of the Chesapeake: The Story of Fort Monroe*. Shippensburg, PA: White Mane Publishing Co., 1989.

Barefoot, Daniel N. *General Robert F. Hoke*. Winston-Salem, NC: John F. Blair, Publisher, 1996.

Bridger, Hal. *Lee's Maverick General: Daniel Harvey Hill*. New York: McGraw-Hill, 1961.

Casdorph, Paul D. *Prince John Magruder: His Life and Campaigns*. New York: John Wiley and Sons, 1996.

Chapman, Craig S. *More Terrible Than Victory: North Carolina's Bloody Bethel Regiment 1861–1865*. London: Brassey's, Inc., 1998.

Faust, Patricia, ed. *Historical Times Illustrated Encyclopedia of the Civil War*. New York, 1980.

Freeman, Douglas Southall. *Lee's Lieutenants*. 3 vols. New York: Charles Scribner's Sons, 1944.

Hale, Laura Virginia. *Four Valiant Years*. Front Royal, VA, 1986.

Holzman, Robert S. *Stormy Ben Butler*. New York: Collier Books, 1961.

Jensen, Les. *32nd Virginia Infantry*. Lynchburg, VA: H.E. Howard, Inc., 1993.

Jordan, David M. *Happiness Is Not My Companion: The Life of General G. K. Warren*. Indianapolis: Indiana University Press, 2001.

Martin, Samuel J. *Kill-Cavalry: The Life of Union General Hugh Judson Kilpatrick.* Mechanicsburg, PA: Stackpole Books, 2000.

Nolan, Dick. *Benjamin Franklin Butler: The Damnedest Yankee.* Novato, CA: Presidio Press, 1991.

Quarstein, John V. *CSS* Virginia*: Mistress of Hampton Roads.* Lynchburg, VA: H.E. Howard, Inc., 2001.

———. *Hampton and Newport News in the Civil War.* Lynchburg, VA: H.E. Howard, Inc., 1998.

Settles, Thomas M. *John Bankhead Magruder.* Baton Rouge: Louisiana State University, 2009.

Shackleford, George. *George Wythe Randolph and the Confederate Elite.* Athens: University of Georgia Press, 1988.

Southwick, Thomas P. *A Duryee Zouave.* Brookneal, VA: Schroeder Publications, 1995.

Wallace, Lee A., Jr. *The Richmond Howitzers.* Lynchburg, VA: H.E. Howard, Inc., 1993.

Wellman, Manly Wade. *Rebel Boast: First at Bethel—Last at Appomattox.* New York: Henry Holt and Company, 1956.

Werlich, Robert. *"Beast" Butler: The Incredible Career of Major General Benjamin Franklin Butler.* Washington, D.C.: Quaker Press, 1962.

Woodworth, Steven E. *Davis and Lee at War.* Lawrence: University Press of Kansas, 1995.

Index

About the Author

John V. Quarstein is an award-winning historian, preservationist and author. He presently serves as historian for the city of Hampton. He previously worked as the director of the Virginia War Museum and as consultant to The Mariners' Museum's *Monitor* Center.

Quarstein is the author of a dozen books, including *Fort Monroe: The Key to the South, CSS* Virginia*: Mistress of Hampton Roads* and *A History of Ironclads: The Power of Iron Over Wood*. His most recent work is *The Monitor Boys: The Crew of the Union's First Ironclad*. He also has produced, narrated and written several PBS documentaries, including *Jamestown: Foundations of Freedom* and the film series *Civil War in Hampton Roads*, which was awarded a 2007 Silver Telly. His latest film, *Hampton: From the Sea to the Stars*, was a 2011 Bronze Telly winner.

John Quarstein is the recipient of the National Trust for Historic Preservation's 1993 President's Award for Historic Preservation; the Civil War Society's Preservation Award in 1996; and the United Daughters of the Confederacy's Jefferson Davis Gold Medal in 1999. Besides his lifelong interest in Tidewater Virginia's Civil War experience, Quarstein is also an avid duck hunter and decoy collector. He lives on Old Point Comfort in Hampton, Virginia, and on his family's Eastern Shore farm near Chestertown, Maryland.

Visit us at
www.historypress.net